RANGERS

THE WADDELL YEARS

1938 – 1984

RANGERS

THE WADDELL YEARS

1938 – 1984

BY

STEPHEN HALLIDAY

First published in Great Britain in 1999 by Chameleon Books under licence from
The Rangers Football Club plc
Chameleon Books is an imprint of André Deutsch Limited
76 Dean Street
London W1V 5HA
HYPERLINK http://www.vci.co.uk

Published in association with the Memorabilia Pack Company
16 Forth Street
Edinburgh EH1 3LH

Printed in Hong Kong by Dah Hua Printing Press Co. Ltd

A catalogue record for this book is available from the British Library

ISBN 0 233 99447 5

ACKNOWLEDGEMENTS

My thanks to John Greig, Peter McCloy, Sandy Jardine and Willie Johnston of Rangers' European Cup-Winners' Cup-winning team for their time, assistance and insight into life under Willie Waddell; to my dad for his constant help and encouragement; and to the staff of the Mitchell Library for their unfailing help and courtesy with my research into an incredible football man's career. Finally, and most importantly, thank you to my wife Ange and sons Chris and Craig for their support and endurance during the many late nights I spent ignoring them in front of the word processor in order to meet the deadline. Hopefully it was worth it.

The Memorabilia Pack Company would like to thank the following people for their assistance: John Smith, the *Daily Record*, Hilda Waddell, Lindsay Hutchison, Stuart Marshall (Kollectables, Glasgow), Mr and Mrs Willie Woodburn, The Scottish Football Association, Trevor Clydesdale, Rangers Football Club and David Mason.

PICTURE ACKNOWLEDGEMENTS

COVER PHOTOGRAPHS
© D.C. Thomson & Co. Ltd.; Eric McCowat Photography.

© D.C. Thomson & Co. Ltd.: 1, 2, 9, 13, 14, 23, 26, 31, 32, 34, 37, 42, 44, 47, 51, 78, 80,85, 86, 87, 88, 89, 91; Eric McCowat Photography: 52, 56,57, 58, 60, 62, 65, 66, 69, 70, 71, 72, 73, 74, 75, 76, 77; © MSI: 35, 49, 50; Popperfoto: 17, 22; Daily Herald Archive NMPFT/Science and Society Picture Library: 10, 18, 19; Sportapics Ltd NMPFT/Science and Society Picture Library: 45, 46; Courtesy of Willie Woodburn: 21, 25, 28.

CONTENTS

INTRODUCTION

No country in world football has made such a significant and celebrated contribution to the cult of the football manager as has Scotland. Jock Stein, Matt Busby and Bill Shankly have come to be revered throughout British, and indeed world football for their achievements. All three emerged from humble Scottish backgrounds to set new standards in football club management. Stein, with Celtic and Scotland, Busby at Manchester United and Shankly with his beloved Liverpool all became powerful, almost mystical figures whose personalities dominated the huge clubs they managed. In later years, the influence of Scottish managers on the fabric of the British game has been maintained by men like Alex Ferguson, George Graham, Kenny Dalglish and Tommy Docherty. Ferguson, like Stein, achieved the feat of winning a European trophy while in charge of a Scottish club. Only one other manager has done that. Sandwiched between Stein's European Cup triumph of 1967 with Celtic and Ferguson's 1983 European Cup-Winners' Cup victory at Aberdeen, William Tweedie Waddell delivered the Cup-Winners' Cup to Rangers.

On the way to defeating Moscow Dynamo 3-2 in the final in Barcelona on 24 May 1972, Rangers knocked out teams from France, Portugal, Italy and West Germany.

It stands as one of the most impressive European successes by any British club, because of the standard of opposition faced in every round.

Yet Willie Waddell has seldom been accorded the same legendary status as Stein, Busby or Shankly.

Why? Perhaps it is because he spent less than three years in the Rangers hot seat before handing over the reins immediately after his triumph in Barcelona. Perhaps it is because he turned down several offers to follow Busby and Shankly into football management in England.

Of all the great managers of his era it was Waddell who enjoyed the most successful playing career and he was certainly the most talented performer on the field. But what really made Waddell different was his total devotion to one club. His passion for Rangers never faltered, even during the periods of his unique career in which they were parted.

Waddell's extraordinary success in his first managerial job at Kilmarnock is often overlooked. He made the Ayrshire club a power in Scottish football and, against all odds, took them to the Scottish League championship title in 1965.

That alone would be enough to guarantee a place in the hall of fame. But Waddell's crowning glory, and the one which gave him most pleasure, came seven years later in Barcelona.

Tempted back into management, in 1969, after a highly successful career in journalism with the *Scottish Daily Express*, Waddell was reunited with the first and only true love of his football life. Rangers were in a mess on and off the pitch but Waddell was able to mount a rescue operation which ultimately ended Celtic's and Jock Stein's total dominance.

For Rangers and their supporters, Waddell will always be remembered as the

man who delivered the much coveted European trophy to the club. But the Waddell years were about so much more that, as this book will attempt to show. It is doubtful if any individual has contributed as much to one club as Waddell did to Rangers, as player, manager, general manager, vice-chairman and managing director.

The stunning Ibrox stadium in which today's team try to attain further triumphs is a remarkable testament to Waddell's foresight and energy. It is a remarkable legacy from a remarkable football man.

Willie Waddell's contribution to Rangers on and off the pitch is without parallel in the club's history.

CHAPTER ONE
WADDELL – THE PLAYER

THE SMALL VILLAGE OF FORTH IN LANARKSHIRE IS AN UNREMARKABLE PLACE BY ANY standards. But it produced, for Scottish football in general, and Rangers Football Club in particular, one of the most important and influential figures of all time.

Willie Waddell was just fifteen years old when his father, a decent full-back with local junior side Forth Wanderers, turned up unexpectedly at Lanark Grammar School. The youngster was taken out of his classroom and informed he was going to Glasgow to play in a trial match for Rangers. The game against Partick Thistle at Firhill, in 1936, was the first time the dumbstruck teenager had ever been to the big city but Waddell, who had made his early reputation with Harthill-based juvenile side Eastfield Heatherbell, helping them to win the coveted Lord Weir Cup in the Lanarkshire region three years in a row, hugely impressed Rangers in the match.

The Ibrox club's legendary manager Bill Struth soon made his move. In an interview which lasted all of five minutes, the pacy young winger with an eye for goal, though still a schoolboy, was offered and accepted a place at Rangers for £2 a week. Waddell was informed that if he could get more money elsewhere, he was welcome to take it. Interestingly, he had actually been offered £6 a week by Portsmouth, then a major power in English football, just a few days earlier. However, there was no competition as far as Waddell was concerned and he duly signed on the dotted line for Rangers. He later recalled, 'I was from a wee mining village and when you left there, it was like coming off a reservation. I saw something in Rangers, there was a pride, a tradition that I felt deep inside me.' It was the start of an extraordinary relationship between club and player which lasted until the day he died in 1992.

Waddell spent two years learning his trade and honing the skills which would make him one of Scottish football's all-time greats before making his first-team debut for Rangers. Firstly, he was farmed out to Strathclyde Juniors and Forth Wanderers, which enabled him to add a physical dimension to his undoubted ability on the ball. A series of sparkling displays in the Rangers reserve side, where he outshone many more experienced players, convinced Struth his prodigy was ready for the big time.

When Waddell did finally step onto the main stage, he could hardly have done so in more spectacular style or dramatic circumstances. At that time, Rangers and Arsenal were the two dominant forces at their respective ends of

> 'I was from a wee mining village and when you left there, it was like coming off a reservation. I saw something in Rangers, there was a pride, a tradition that I felt deep inside me.'

Proudly wearing the blue jersey which he filled with style and distinction.

British football and regular matches were arranged between the two. It was at the 1938 version of the unofficial 'Battle of Britain' that Struth decided to unleash his new discovery. On 29 August 1938 a crowd of 41,000 took their places at Ibrox to see Rangers take on Arsenal that Monday night. Rangers were desperate for victory as they had failed to win any of the three previous meetings between the teams. Waddell, who had scored twice in a 6–1 win for the reserves over St Mirren at the stadium the previous Friday night, was the surprise name in the squad. He had only signed professional forms five months earlier, on his seventeenth birthday, an event which had been noted by the newspapers. Waverley, the respected football correspondent of the *Daily Record*, had written: 'One can readily understand Manager Struth not wasting any time in making this youngster an Ibrox fixture. He is too good a proposition to take risks with.'

Waddell received the unexpected call to face the English giants thanks to injuries suffered by established front men Bobby Main and Alex Venters. To make it all the more daunting for the debutant, filling the right-wing role for Arsenal was the Welsh superstar of the time, Bryn Jones. Jones had just been signed by the Gunners from Wolves for a then staggering fee of £14,000 and had scored on his debut against Portsmouth two days earlier. Many of the big crowd had come along simply to see Jones whose presence made up for several other notable absentees in the Arsenal line-up. But Jones was overshadowed on the night as Waddell made a dream debut, scoring the only goal of the match.

The glory strike came in the

An idol for young Rangers fans of the time, Waddell is captured as part of a football card collection.

Willie Waddell

Copyright SUNDAY MAIL JUNIOR SPORTS CLUB *Photograph*

TELEPHONE:
IBROX 159

W. R. SIMPSON, C.A.
SECRETARY

FOUNDED

THE RANGERS FC

IBROX PARK

REGISTE

Head down, preparing to beat another full-back and deliver a telling cross.

To add to his trickery on the deck Waddell was a fine header of the ball.

TELEGRAMS:
IBROX PARK
GLASGOW

Wᴹ STRUTH
MANAGER

TBALL CLUB LTD

FFICE:
ASGOW · S · W · 1

Waddell's right boot sends another precise cross towards a grateful team-mate.

twenty-fifth minute as Waddell displayed maturity and tenacity beyond his years to drive the ball beyond the outstanding Arsenal keeper, George Swindin, at the second attempt. He was unfortunate not to score a second but Swindin denied him with a fine save. Even so, Willie Waddell had well and truly announced his arrival as a Rangers player.

The legendary Ibrox captain Davie Meiklejohn, who won a phenomenal twelve league championships and five Scottish Cups in his career at the club, was certain his old boss Struth was on to a winner. A columnist with the *Daily Record* following his retirement in 1936, Meiklejohn wrote of Waddell's debut: 'He paid his way.' But the hard-to-please 'Meek' did have some advice to hand out to the new boy. 'If I have one fault against him,' Meiklejohn went on, 'it is in not using his speed when left with a clear field. However, it was a big match for the youngster and he did exceedingly well.'

Waddell's performance in the game confirmed him as one of the key figures in the rebuilding process being undertaken by Struth. Rangers had finished just third in the Scottish League the previous season, a failure Struth was not familiar with having won six of the previous eight titles. But now some of the great names of the era had reached the end of the line and Struth knew he needed younger blood in order to reassert his club's dominance. Along with Waddell, in came full-back Jock 'Tiger' Shaw and striker Willie Thornton. All three players would make an indelible imprint on the club's history.

After that superb start against Arsenal, Waddell simply could not be left out of the Rangers first team. He retained his place for the visit of Ayr United on league business five days later, on 3 September 1938. He didn't score this time but was happy enough with his performance in a 4–1 win over the men from Somerset Park. Waddell went on to make twenty-seven league appearances in that 1938–9 season as the championship was won by an eleven-point margin over second-placed Celtic. He scored seven goals in total, and in addition to collecting a championship medal, helped Rangers lift the then highly prestigious Charity Cup on 13 May 1939 as Third Lanark were beaten in front of almost 30,000 fans in the Hampden final.

Waddell's 'Old Firm' debut proved to be another remarkable occasion. The match, at Ibrox on 2 January 1939, still has a place in the record books today – courtesy of the crowd of 118,730 who squeezed into the stadium to watch it. It remains the biggest attendance ever for an 'Old Firm' contest, or indeed for any Scottish league match. Some 30,000 more were believed to have been locked out as Rangers looked to avenge the humiliating 6–2 defeat they had suffered at the hands of their greatest rivals at Parkhead earlier in the season. Goals from Dave Kinnear and Alex Venters were enough to give Rangers a 2–1 win on this occasion and Waddell won widespread praise for his contribution.

Waddell's pedigree as a top-class player had quickly become obvious to everyone and a glorious few years surely lay ahead. However, like many other gifted footballers of his generation, he was to find his ambitions put on the back burner as the world faced its darkest hour. The 1939–40 league season was just five games old – Waddell had played in every one for an unbeaten Rangers, scoring two goals – when the Second World War broke out. Competition ceased and Rangers supremo Struth set about ensuring his players made their contribution to the war effort, either on active service or in munitions factories and the Clydeside shipyards.

The young Waddell found himself engaged as an electrician at the famous Harland & Wolff yard but he was still able to play football on a regular basis for Rangers in the revamped wartime leagues. Entertainment for the public during the hostilities was clearly important and stars like Waddell did their bit on the football field, helping Rangers to dominate the various competitions. The club won twenty-five of the thirty-four trophies up for grabs during the seven seasons before normal service was resumed at home and abroad.

During the war, English legends such as Stanley Matthews guested for various clubs around the country, including Rangers and it was at around this time that comparisons started to be made between the brilliant Matthews, his England rival and friend Tom Finney and Waddell himself. Willie Thornton, Waddell's team-mate and great friend for so many years on and off the pitch, was able to offer a rare insight into the debate as he had played centre-forward alongside all three wingers. When asked who was the best, he replied, 'I played with Finney in some of the Army games during the war and alongside Matthews in a match for Rangers. Of course, I also saw Matthews in action for his country on plenty of occasions against Scotland and once when we faced each other in an international at Hampden. But Waddell was equal to them both and, in my opinion, better. He was better simply because he had the ability to do the unexpected. You could hear the buzz of anticipation from the crowd when he got the ball. We had a good understanding when we played together. It was never something we worked on, it just came right for us when we played.'

Probably the most famous match Waddell played for Rangers came

'He was better simply because he had the ability to do the unexpected. You could hear the buzz of anticipation from the crowd when he got the ball.'

towards the end of the wartime period when Moscow Dynamo visited Ibrox as part of their British tour. The Russians carried an air of mystery which fascinated the Scottish public and 95,000 descended on Govan for the 28 November 1945 fixture. The game lived up to all expectations. Waddell had an early penalty brilliantly saved by the fabled Dynamo keeper Tiger Khomich and Rangers then found themselves 2–0 down. But Scottish grit proved a match for Russian flair in the second half, as well as Russian gamesmanship. At one point Dynamo managed to send a substitute on to the pitch without actually removing a player. Remarkably, the referee failed to spot the extra man, though the alert figure of Torry Gillick was able to quickly count to 12 and the Rangers forward brought Dynamo's extra man to the official's attention. Goals from Jimmy Smith and George Young earned a draw.

Official Scottish League football resumed in 1946–7 and, as Rangers looked to take their pre-war Scottish football supremacy into the immediate post-war period, Waddell played a priceless part in the success which came to Ibrox.

Rangers had a new rival – a vibrant Hibs side, whose attacking brilliance was borne out of a front line which became known as the 'Famous Five' – Gordon Smith, Bobby Johnstone, Lawrie Reilly, Eddie Turnbull and Willie Ormond. Nonetheless Rangers won the championship by two points from the Edinburgh men, Waddell chipping in with five goals from twenty-two appearances and creating many of the eighteen goals scored by Thornton.

The crowds were rolling back as the country savoured the return to peace and games between Rangers and Hibs were hugely popular, eclipsing even the Old Firm fixtures. A staggering 125,154 were at Hampden on 22 March 1947 to see Rangers beat their Edinburgh rivals 3–1 in the semi-final of the inaugural League Cup tournament. Waddell sealed victory for Rangers with a stunning shot from a tight angle but unfortunately missed the 4–0 final win over Aberdeen because of injury.

The following season, Hibs turned the tables in the league championship with a two-point winning margin over Rangers. All in all, 1947–8 was a disappointment for Waddell as injury restricted him to just twelve league appearances and also robbed him of a place in the Scottish Cup Final where Rangers beat Morton after a replay.

Injuries were something of an occupational hazard throughout his career, his blurring and sudden bursts of pace causing him to pull muscles on many occasions. The season had its moments for him however, most notably in the semi-final of the Scottish Cup when a British record crowd of 143,570 were at Hampden to see Rangers beat Hibs 1–0. The only goal was typical of Waddell's priceless partnership with Thornton as the winger surged down the right before sending over an inch-perfect cross which was bulleted beyond Hibs keeper George Farm by the fearless centre-forward's head.

The season also had its compensations for Waddell off the pitch. In February, Rangers travelled to Lisbon for a friendly against Benfica and, apart from contributing to an impressive 3–0 win for the Scots, Waddell also met Hilda, his future wife, on the trip, an air hostess on the team's plane. The meeting sparked a glorious period of Waddell's playing career as he established himself in the Scotland side

'Nature bestowed all his gifts with a smile;
His left foot, his right foot, his noddle;
When you can buy all these wonderful things,
Then you can buy Willie Waddell;
Deedle, dawdle, Willie Waddell.'

and in 1948–9 helped Rangers win the first 'Treble' in Scottish football history.

This was the season when the fabled 'Iron Curtain' defence of keeper Bobby Brown, full-backs George Young and Jock Shaw and half-backs Ian McColl, Willie Woodburn and Sammy Cox came into its own. At times, their remarkable consistency in keeping the opposition out overshadowed the efforts of gifted attacking players like Waddell, Thornton and Torry Gillick.

The Ibrox fans were in no doubts about their real hero, a player they nicknamed 'The Deedle'. It was a monicker which would stick with Waddell for the rest of his life. It was derived from rhyming slang in a song the Rangers fans sang about their jet-heeled winger. The song went: 'Nature bestowed all his gifts with a smile; His left foot, his right foot, his noddle; When you can buy all these wonderful things, Then you can buy Willie Waddell; Deedle, dawdle, Willie Waddell.'

The League Cup was the first trophy 'Deedle' and his team-mates collected in that all-conquering season. Rangers finished top of a ferociously competitive qualifying section ahead of Celtic and Hibs which all boiled down to an Old Firm decider at Ibrox in front of 105,000 fans. Waddell sent the home support into delirium when he scored eighteen minutes from time to give Rangers a 2–1 win. He subsequently played in the quarter-final and semi-final victories over St Mirren and Dundee, only for his injury jinx to strike again and force him to sit out the March final when Rangers beat Raith Rovers 2–0 at Hampden.

Another trophy-laden Rangers side of the post-war era. Waddell is second on the extreme left of the back row next to his mentor, the legendary Bill Struth.

The second leg of the treble triumph brought Waddell more personal satisfaction as he played in every round of the Scottish Cup campaign. The final against Clyde on 23 April 1949, witnessed by another massive Hampden crowd of 120,162, was the scene of one of his finest displays in a light blue shirt. Waddell was the architect of a convincing 4–1 win for Rangers, his perfect cross for Billy Williamson to head the favourites into a 2–0 interval lead the crunch moment of the contest.

A week later, Cliftonhill provided the backdrop for Rangers to complete the set as they regained the championship. Going into that final day of the season, Dundee led Rangers by a point and with their superior goal average they needed only a draw against Falkirk to take the title. But the Dens Park men crashed to a shock 4–1 defeat and Rangers took full advantage, the Waddell-Thornton alliance paying dividends as the centre-forward grabbed a hat-trick in a 4–1 win over already relegated Albion Rovers.

Waddell rated scoring the title-clinching goal of 1953 as the sweetest moment of his playing career.

Rangers were champions again in 1949–50 but there was no medal for Waddell this time, injury restricting him to a mere seven appearances and also ruling him out of the Scottish Cup Final win over East Fife. If nothing else, the season allowed him to show his versatility when he filled in for the injured Thornton as centre-forward in a League Cup tie against Celtic and duly scored Rangers' second goal in a 2–0 win.

Waddell was back, fully fit and a permanent fixture once more, in 1950–51 but now it was Rangers as a whole who were ailing. They surrendered the championship, finishing ten points behind Hibs and the Easter Road club also ended Rangers' interest in the Scottish Cup in a titanic second-round contest watched by 102,342 at Ibrox.

Although Waddell moved into his thirties in 1951 he remained an influential figure in the Rangers line-up and his hunger for success was as keen as ever. However, it was unfulfilled in 1951–2 as Rangers flopped in all three competitions, having to settle for second best to Hibs in the championship again, this time by four points.

But glory would come Waddell's way again as a player, for the last time as it turned out, the following season. After an awful start to the campaign which saw them lose 5–0 to Hearts at Tynecastle in a League Cup sectional tie, Rangers recovered to win the Double. They beat Aberdeen 1–0 in the Scottish Cup Final replay at Hampden and then a week later they claimed the league title. Nine points behind at one stage, they produced a storming finish to go into the final day needing just a draw against Queen of the South at

Keeping it in the family as Waddell gets ready for another trip abroad on football business.

Palmerston Park to lift the title on goal average from Hibs. It looked grim for Rangers as they trailed 1–0 in Dumfries but, with fifteen minutes remaining, Waddell emerged as the hero. He drilled in the equalizer and, in so doing, earned himself the final winner's medal of his playing career. Waddell later described this goal as the sweetest moment of his playing career with the club, saying, 'Nothing is better than scoring the goal which makes Rangers champions.'

Rangers then entered a period of transition and although Waddell remained for three more seasons, he became an increasingly peripheral figure in the squad. In April 1954 Bill Struth announced his decision to stand down as manager after thirty-four prolifically successful years in the job. Struth had been the biggest influence on Waddell and when Scot Symon, Waddell's former team-mate who had forged a glowing managerial reputation with East Fife and Preston North End, took over in the summer it was clear there would be major changes at Ibrox.

Waddell played fifteen first-team games during Symon's first season at the club, another barren affair, but in 1955–6 he found himself in the reserves as his right-wing berth was taken by Alex Scott, a worthy successor. On 12 October 1955 (just over seventeen years after his debut against Arsenal) Willie Waddell's first-team career at Rangers ended. Again, it was against English opposition as Rangers travelled south to play Manchester City in a friendly. Waddell was drafted in to play at outside-left when Johnny Hubbard failed to make it back in time from an international match between the Scottish and Danish Leagues in Copenhagen the previous evening. Suitably enough, Waddell ended on a winning note as goals from Sammy Baird and John Queen earned Rangers a 2–1 win under the Maine Road floodlights.

While Symon steered Rangers to the 1955–6 championship, there were rumours in the second eleven that Waddell was poised to join St Mirren. But he simply could not contemplate playing for another club and when he was handed a free transfer at the end of the campaign, Waddell decided to retire.

It was the end of a career in which, including wartime appearances, he had played 601 first-team games for Rangers. But for Waddell the Ranger, that would be only half the story.

WADDELL'S INTERNATIONAL RECORD

WARTIME AND VICTORY INTERNATIONALS (Scotland's scores on left)

18 April 1942	England 5–4	(Hampden)
10 October 1942	England 0–0	(Wembley)
17 April 1943	England 0–4	(Hampden)
16 October 1943	England 0–8	(Maine Road)
14 April 1945	England 1–6	(Hampden)
12 November 1945	Wales 2–0	(Hampden)
2 February 1946	Northern Ireland 3–2	(Belfast)
13 April 1946	England 1–0	(Hampden)
15 May 1946	Switzerland 3–1	(Hampden)
12 August 1946	England 2–2	(Maine Road)

FULL INTERNATIONALS

19 October 1946	Wales 1–3	(Wrexham)
23 October 1948	Wales 3–1	(Cardiff)
17 November 1948	Northern Ireland 3–2	(Hampden)
9 April 1949	England 3–1	(Wembley)
27 April 1949	France 2–0	(Hampden)
1 October 1949	Northern Ireland 8–2	(Belfast)
15 April 1950	England 0–1	(Hampden)
14 April 1951	England 3–2	(Wembley)
12 May 1951	Denmark 3–1	(Hampden)
16 May 1951	France 1–0	(Hampden)
20 May 1951	Belgium 5–0	(Brussels)
27 May 1951	Austria 0–4	(Vienna)
6 October 1951	Northern Ireland 3–0	(Belfast)
14 November 1951	Wales 0–1	(Hampden)
3 October 1953	Northern Ireland 3–1	(Belfast)
16 October 1954	Wales 1–0	(Cardiff)
3 November 1954	Northern Ireland 2–2	(Hampden)

Waddell also played in several representative matches for the Scottish League.

CHAPTER TWO

WADDELL – THE INTERNATIONAL

WHILE WILLIE WADDELL'S NAME WILL ALWAYS BE SYNONYMOUS WITH RANGERS, IT WAS not just as a club player that he made a telling contribution to Scottish football, although as with his domestic career, Waddell's international achievements were stymied by the Second World War. Nonetheless he was a Scotland player of considerable note, representing his country seventeen times in official internationals and in nine wartime matches.

The clamour for top-level football entertainment to offset the austerity and depression of the war was amply illustrated by the crowd of 91,000 on the slopes of Hampden for Waddell's first game in a Scotland shirt, against England on 18 April 1942. Just as his debut for Rangers had been a dramatic affair, so too were the circumstances the first time he pulled on the dark blue of Scotland.

Preparing to face the Auld Enemy. George Young is doing the introductions. Willie Waddell, extreme right, waits his turn.

Waddell lined up in his familiar right-wing role in a side which, as it turned out, contained two other men who would join him as managerial greats of the post-war era. Preston North End skipper Bill Shankly and Matt Busby of Liverpool were both in the half-back line as Scotland thrilled the home fans with a 5–4 win at Hampden. Blackpool striker Jock Dodds was the hero with a hat-trick and Waddell's fellow debutant, the great Billy Liddell, also scored.

That victory, however, was a precious rarity for the Scots in the regular wartime series of matches against the Auld Enemy, six of which featured Waddell. A goalless draw at Wembley later in 1942 was acceptable enough but the following year Waddell felt the pain of two crushing defeats at the hands of the English. Losing 4–0 at Hampden was bad enough but the real misery came at Maine Road on 16 October 1943. The scoreline read England 8 Scotland 0 and Waddell and his team-mates could only marvel at the brilliance of England and four-goal centre-forward Tommy Lawton in particular. Waddell's next appearance was in the final wartime clash with England at Hampden on 14 April 1945, a game watched by a remarkable crowd of 133,000. Sadly for the Scots, they were handed another harsh lesson, a 6–1 defeat.

As part of the celebrations to mark the end of the war the 1945–6 season saw Scotland's fixtures labelled Victory Internationals. As such, they do not count as official internationals but the first of them brought Waddell his first goal for his

country. He opened the scoring in the 2–0 win over Wales at Hampden as Scotland embarked on a run of success to usher in the post-war era.

Another massive crowd – 139,468 – crammed into Hampden on 13 April 1946 as Waddell set up Jimmy Delaney to score the only goal of the game against England.

Waddell also appeared in another unofficial clash with the English later that year, perhaps one of the finest displays of his career, to aid the Bolton Disaster Fund. The match was played to raise funds for the family and dependants of the 33 people killed at Burnden Park on 9 March 1946. A crowd of 85,000, almost 40,000 more than expected, had turned up for an FA Cup quarter-final tie between Bolton Wanderers and Stoke City. When a barrier collapsed at the Railway End of the ground, a crush ensued which saw 33 spectators die and some 500 suffer injuries.

Perhaps inspired by the presence of Stanley Matthews on the opposite side, Waddell was at his irresistible best. The 2–2 draw was a wingers' masterclass, Matthews setting up both English goals to give them a half-time lead and Waddell responding by laying on two for Willie Thornton as the Scots fought back after the break.

The official Home International series resumed in 1946–7 and it brought Waddell his 'proper' Scotland debut, against Wales at Wrexham. He got off to

Scottish goals were unfortunately a rarity against the Auld Enemy during the war years.

'Waddell at least had his first cap, although rationing meant that he had to wait several months to be presented with his international jersey!'

the perfect start, slotting Scotland ahead from the penalty spot, but it was a poor side that season and Wales stormed back to win 3–1. Waddell at least had his first cap, although rationing meant that he had to wait several months to be presented with his international jersey!

He had an even longer wait for his next Scotland appearance. A combination of injury and the SFA's merry-go-round selection policy, as they tried to stumble across a winning blend, meant it was two years before Waddell was called up again. When the chance came, with Wales the opposition once more, he grabbed it in emphatic fashion.

He scored twice in the 3–1 win in Cardiff, the first time Scotland had experienced victory on Welsh soil for seventeen years. He then played in the 3–2 win over Northern Ireland at Hampden which set up a championship decider with England, played on 9 April 1949.

This was one of Scotland's finest Wembley performances and after inspired Morton keeper Jimmy Cowan had somehow defied an opening twenty-minute blitz from England, Waddell and company took centre stage. The Rangers star's right-wing partnership with Jimmy Mason of Third Lanark was a revelation as they forced the English defence on to their heels. Waddell was directly up against Derby County left-back Jack Howe, one of the first footballers ever to play while wearing contact lenses but the Scotland winger was simply a blur to Howe all afternoon. Mason opened the scoring, Billy Steel made it 2–0 and then Waddell provided a superb cross for Lawrie Reilly to put the Scots out of reach. Jackie Milburn's reply for England was no more than an irritation as the Scottish fans celebrated long into the London night. The celebrations continued as Waddell and the other home-based Scots were greeted by a crowd of 10,000 when they returned to Glasgow by train.

Just over two weeks later, a record midweek crowd at Hampden of 130,000 saw the Scottish heroes beat France 2–0. Willie Thornton was the only change to the side who had humbled England, giving Waddell a rare chance to team up with his Ibrox sidekick at international level, an event which happened just four times.

In the summer of 1949, the successful Scots boarded the Queen Mary for a nine-match tour of North America. None of the games counted as official internationals but in a 7–0 win over Philadelphia, Waddell produced a fabulous one-man show. Deputizing at centre-forward for the injury Billy Houliston, he scored six of the Scottish goals.

There was an added edge to the competition when Scotland began their defence of the Home International Championship the following season. For the first time, the competition was to be used as a qualifying group for the World Cup Finals as the British associations had finally seen the light and decided to take part in FIFA's global party. It all got off to the perfect start as Northern

Ireland were swamped 8–2 at Hampden on 1 October 1949, Waddell helping himself to two of Scotland's first-ever World Cup goals. He then missed the 2–0 win over Wales the following month through injury, but was back for the championship decider against England at Hampden on 15 April 1950 when Scotland only needed a draw to retain the championship.

Before the match FIFA generously announced that the top two nations would now be invited to the World Cup Finals in Brazil. For reasons best known to themselves, the SFA threw the offer back in the world governing body's face and grandly stated their team would only be on the plane to Rio if they won the Home International crown. Scotland trailed 1–0 to a Bentley goal and the equalizer simply would not come. Hearts striker Willie Bauld struck the crossbar in a frantic finale and, in the dying seconds, Waddell looked set to clinch Scotland's World Cup berth only for his shot to clear Bert Williams' crossbar by inches. Scotland had finished second.

SFA president John Lamb, backed by Rangers and Scotland skipper George Young, then attempted to persuade the Executive Committee to change their mind and send a team to Brazil in any case. But their representations were ignored by the intransigent SFA secretary George Graham and a gifted Scottish side were left on the outside looking in.

Waddell missed Scotland's next six games before returning to the fold in April 1951 for another successful Wembley mission, a tense and closely fought 3–2 win. He retained his place for Hampden victories over Denmark and France before scoring in his first overseas assignment for Scotland, a 5–0 romp over Belgium in Brussels.

A week later, he got a glimpse of the emergence of a new cynical style of European football. Austria crushed the Scots 4–0 in Vienna with a brutal display which bordered on thuggery. In the opening minute, Waddell was sent hurtling six feet over the touchline by the Austrian left-back and that set the tone for a shameful ninety minutes.

Waddell's international appearances then became more sporadic and in 1954 he again missed out on a place in the World Cup Finals, held in Switzerland, even though Scotland this time accepted FIFA's invitation after finishing runners-up to England in the qualifying table. He missed out because there were no Rangers players in the squad as they were required for a club trip to the USA that summer – a situation hard to imagine now. In all probability Waddell had little difficulty coming to terms with the club's decision. For him, Rangers always came first. At least he had the consolation of having contributed to Scotland's qualification, as he had played in the 3–1 win over Northern Ireland in Belfast.

The SFA bore no grudge towards the Ibrox players and on 3 November 1954 Waddell was called up for official Scotland duty for the seventeenth and last time, an undistinguished 2–2 draw with Northern Ireland at Hampden. He left with a proud record of having scored six goals in his seventeen full internationals – twelve wins, one draw and just four defeats.

Waddell scored in Scotland's first ever World Cup tie but never played in the Finals.

CHAPTER THREE
WADDELL – THE MANAGER

WHEN WILLIE WADDELL LEFT IBROX HE HAD NO INTENTION OF FOLLOWING MANY OF HIS Rangers contemporaries into football management. Instead, he decided to pour his energies into a new career in journalism and he proved a successful columnist with the now defunct *Glasgow Evening Citizen.*

Just over a year after calling a halt to his playing days, however, Waddell made a dramatic return to Scottish football. On 19 July 1957 he was named as the new manager of Kilmarnock. The Ayrshire club were an emerging force, having lost in the final of the Scottish Cup a few months earlier, but they had been rocked by the resignation of Malcolm MacDonald as boss in the summer.

MacDonald left to join Brentford and at an angry shareholders' meeting, the Rugby Park board was asked what it intended to do about the situation. The board members' answer was to persuade Waddell to put away his notebook and take on the challenge of bringing silverware to the club. What Waddell went on to achieve in eight seasons in charge at Rugby Park was arguably as great a feat as he managed in any other part of his career.

> **'What Waddell went on to achieve in eight seasons in charge at Rugby Park was arguably as great a feat as he managed in any other part of his career.'**

On the morning of his first match as Killie boss, a League Cup sectional tie against Hearts at Rugby Park, Waddell received a telegram from Willie Thornton, now manager of Dundee. 'Best of luck...will meet you on Wednesday, joint top of our section,' read his old pal's message. On 10 August 1957 Thornton's words came true as Kilmarnock beat Hearts 2–1 and Dundee swamped Queen's Park 5–2. Waddell's men then beat Dundee, winning 3–0 at Dens Park.

There was nothing spectacular about the first two seasons at the Rugby Park helm, although he gave Rangers an early indication of his prowess by guiding his new team to a 4–3 win at Ibrox in his first League game as a manager. Waddell took time to shape and build a side which combined durability and flair and in the 1959–60 season Kilmarnock started to come good. They emerged from the pack to provide a tremendous challenge to Hearts in the title race, finally losing out to the great Tynecastle side of the time by just four points. Kilmarnock were also runners-up in the Scottish Cup, losing 2–0 to Rangers in a Hampden final watched by 108,000.

Suddenly, the provincial club were the talk of Scottish football and Waddell's managerial stock was on the rise. He persuaded the Kilmarnock board to sanction full-time football and Waddell's unforgiving training methods,

Waddell, pictured alongside club and international team-mates, was always a keen student of worldwide football.

implemented brilliantly by his sidekick Walter McCrae, put the accent firmly on pushing his players to the physical limit during training. There was no place for slackers and the Ayrshire men became one of the fittest teams in the country.

They were rewarded for their double near-miss when the Scottish League nominated Killie to represent their country in the International Soccer League Championship being promoted by the United States Soccer Federation. The competition was part of a bid to promote the sport in the US and Waddell's men found themselves among illustrious company in the summer of 1960. They were drawn in Group One alongside German giants Bayern Munich, English champions Burnley, Nice from France, a US representative side and Northern Ireland's Glenavon, whilst the other group featured Red Star Belgrade, Sampdoria, Rapid Vienna, Sporting Lisbon, IFK Norkopping and Brazilian champions Bangu.

Waddell took his first managerial brush with foreign opposition seriously and it was to make a lasting impression on him. In their opening match at the New York Polo Grounds, Killie came from behind to beat Bayern 3–1. Their performance won lavish praise with the *New York Herald Tribune* newspaper stating, 'This was soccer at its best.'

Glenavon were brushed aside 2–0, as were Burnley in a satisfying 'Battle of Britain' triumph. A 1–1 draw with Nice and a 3–1 win over the hosts meant Kilmarnock won their section and were in the final. They had the bulk of the 25,000 New York crowd behind them as they took on Bangu for the trophy on 6 August 1960 but a combination of Brazilian brilliance and a Big Apple heatwave proved too much for the Scots and they lost 2–0. They had done their country proud, however, and for Waddell it had been a valuable learning process.

Young players flourished under Waddell at Rugby Park and in the 1960–61 season, the club's progress was maintained although Killie again had to settle for runners-up prizes. Rangers edged them out on two fronts this time, by a solitary point in the championship race and with a 2–0 win in the League Cup Final. However, Waddell had now established Kilmarnock as consistent contenders for silverware. All that remained was to take the final step and lift a major trophy – something the club had not achieved since 1929.

But there was final heartache again in 1962 when Killie faced Hearts in the League Cup Final at Hampden. It was a controversial affair as referee Tom 'Tiny' Wharton angered the Kilmarnock fans by mysteriously ruling out a Frank Beattie header in the final minute of the match that would have made the score 1–1. There seemed to be nothing wrong with Beattie's 'equalizer' but Wharton thought that the Kilmarnock player had handled the ball. It was a sickening blow for Waddell and his players in a season which also saw them finish runners-up in the championship again.

When Kilmarnock suffered that by now familiar feeling in 1963–64, this time finishing six points behind champions Rangers, it seemed as though the trophy Waddell so desperately craved was destined to elude him. But the script which unfolded for Waddell and the Rugby Park club in 1964–65 was to wipe away the 'nearly men' tag in extraordinary fashion.

Midway through the season, Waddell had made the stunning announcement that he was going to resign as manager at the end of the campaign. Despite the best efforts of the Killie board to persuade him to stay, Waddell, unbeknown to anyone outside his immediate family and friends, sought a return to journalism. Despite this disruption it remained a season to

> 'Waddell took his first managerial brush with foreign opposition seriously and it was to make a lasting impression on him. In their opening match at the New York Polo Grounds, Killie came from behind to beat Bayern 3–1. Their performance won lavish praise with the *New York Herald Tribune* newspaper stating, "This was soccer at its best".'

> 'Midway through the season, Waddell had made the stunning announcement that he was going to resign as manager at the end of the campaign.'

savour for the Kilmarnock fans, starting off with a never-to-be forgotten European showdown with Eintracht Frankfurt. Waddell was a keen student of European football and in 1963 he had travelled to Italy with Jock Stein, then the manager of Dunfermline, on a trip sponsored by the *Scottish Daily Express*. The two brightest emerging managers in Scotland went to study the training and coaching methods of Helenio Herrera at Inter Milan. Herrera was considered the undisputed master of European football, having introduced the famed catenaccio defensive system and his influence was to have a profound effect on both Waddell and Stein. Stein later reflected, 'What impressed Willie and I most was the fact Herrera's methods were based on mobility and a lot of ball work. He seemed to concentrate on quick usage and familiarity with the ball.'

The Eintracht clash was Waddell's first major chance to try out his own ideas on the European stage. The Germans were still revered in Scotland for their magnificent supporting role to the mighty Real Madrid in the classic European Cup Final at Hampden four years earlier. Real Madrid won the game 7–3. When Killie were drawn against them in the first round of the Fairs Cup, it looked like a mismatch and that analysis appeared to be justified when Eintracht won the first leg 3–0 in Frankfurt. Waddell, never afraid to experiment, had tried out a 4–2–4 system in the match but it simply hadn't come off on the night. Nonetheless he persisted with it in domestic games and his players started to get to grips with the formation. Still, the second leg against Eintracht at Rugby Park on 22 September 1964 was not expected to be of anything more than academic interest to the home fans.

When a thirty-yard thunderbolt ripped past Killie keeper Campbell Forsyth in the second minute to make it 4–0 on aggregate, it seemed there was no way back. But then one of the great European comebacks of all time unfolded in front of the delirious and disbelieving Killie support, Ronnie Hamilton and Brian McIlroy scoring as Waddell's men took command to lead 2–1 at half-time. Seven minutes into the second half, Jim McFadzean scored a third and suddenly Killie were now only 4–3 down overall. It was bedlam at Rugby Park when eight minutes from time Jackie McInally levelled the aggregate score with a stunning header. Astonishingly, the drama wasn't over yet. In the dying seconds, Hamilton made it 5–1 on the night to seal a scarcely credible 5–4 triumph.

Although Kilmarnock went out of the tournament at the hands of a fine Everton side in the next round, the European adventure was used as the springboard to the club's greatest-ever domestic success. Yet another sustained championship challenge was mounted and when it came to the final run-in, it boiled down to a straight battle between Killie and Hearts. As fate would have it, the fixture list saw the teams scheduled to meet each other at Tynecastle on the final day of the campaign. When Kilmarnock arrived in Edinburgh on 24 April 1965 they were two points behind Hearts who only required a draw to take the title. To overturn the goal average advantage Hearts held, Waddell's team needed to win by two clear goals. The home team were odds-on favourites but in arguably the most dramatic finale to a Scottish League championship ever, Kilmarnock duly won 2–0.

After soaking up early Hearts pressure, Davie Sneddon headed a Tommy McLean cross beyond Jim Cruickshank to give Killie a twenty-seventh-minute lead and two minutes later, Hearts were shell shocked when Brian McIlroy grabbed Kilmarnock's second. The Ayrshire men then held on to win the championship by just 0.04 of a goal.

Waddell danced an uncharacteristic jig of joy onto the Tynecastle pitch as he celebrated a truly remarkable success. 'This is the one I wanted more than anything else,' he said, 'and it was my last chance as a manager to lift a major honour. The Scottish Cup would have had more glamour but winning the championship is a greater achievement. My players deserve it, they have made my time with Kilmarnock as happy as any period in my career.'

It was, as they say, a heck of a way to go. But as Waddell departed Rugby Park – despite last-ditch efforts by the Killie board to keep him, including the unprecedented offer of a ten-year contract – he was clearly unaware that his career in management was far from over.

Before then, however, Waddell was to make an altogether different kind of imprint on Scottish football.

Kilmarnock enjoyed unprecedented success under Waddell's leadership.

CHAPTER FOUR
WADDELL – THE JOURNALIST

WADDELL'S DECISION TO QUIT AS KILMARNOCK MANAGER HALFWAY THROUGH THEIR championship-winning season sparked six months of intense speculation as to what he would do next but he consistently insisted he had no definite plans.

When his Rugby Park contract officially terminated on 30 June 1965 all Waddell would say was, 'Right now I am going on a caravanning holiday with my family.' He continued, 'Looking back, in football as in everything else, you tend to remember the triumphs and forget the disappointments. Everything that has gone before seems to be rose-coloured. My greatest pleasure during my time at Rugby Park has been the relationship between myself and my staff. I have a league championship medal from the club but I don't need a medal to remind me of the day at Tynecastle.' It would be three months before Waddell's next port of call would be revealed – a dramatic return to the media.

His association with journalism had started when he was a Rangers player. Each day after training, for five years, he had travelled to Edinburgh to learn his alternative trade at the offices of the *Scottish Daily Mail*. After he had hung up his boots at Ibrox he joined the *Glasgow Evening Citizen* at Albion Street where he worked as a sub-editor and then as a sports columnist. It was to Albion Street that Waddell returned in September 1965, to forge a considerable reputation as a football writer with the then peerless *Scottish Daily Express*.

The front page of the paper on Monday 27 September proclaimed, 'What is the secret of Willie Waddell – look out tomorrow for a special announcement in the *Scottish Daily Express*.' While readers puzzled over which club Waddell would be taking charge of, the next morning they discovered they would be reading his views on their sports pages every day. In his first column Waddell wrote, 'I will give my ideas freely and without bias. Undoubtedly you will disagree sometimes – that is your perogative.' He then provided a warning to his former colleagues in Scottish football that he intended to spare no one in his assessment of their performances. 'I never forgot that without criticism we are all inclined to jog along self-satisfied,' he penned.

In his first column Waddell wrote 'I will give my ideas freely and without bias. Undoubtedly you will disagree sometimes – that is your perogative.'

Waddell quickly established himself as one of Scottish football's must-read sportswriters. He covered top matches at home and abroad, often in tandem with the *Express*'s number-one writer John Mackenzie, who was known as 'The Voice of Football'. From the press box, he witnessed a sea change in Scottish football as the brilliant Celtic side of Jock Stein emerged from a lean period of

Waddell was as direct and successful with a pen as he had been with a football.

their history to cast a shadow over Rangers with the scale of their achievements.

Under Stein, Celtic had won their first trophy for eight years when they lifted the Scottish Cup in 1965. A late-season slump by Rangers then saw Celtic come through in 1965–6 to win the championship for the first time in twelve years. Although Rangers gained a measure of compensation by winning an Old Firm Scottish Cup Final, it was the start of one of the grimmest periods in Ibrox history on the field.

The 1966–7 season was pivotal in the reversal of fortunes experienced by the great rivals. Celtic lifted every domestic honour while Rangers slid to the most humiliating result since their formation, losing 1–0 to tiny Berwick Rangers in the first round of the Scottish Cup. Waddell was not impressed and joined in the general condemnation of the slip in standards at Ibrox. Salvation was available, however, as Rangers reached the final of the European Cup-Winners' Cup where they were to play Bayern Munich the week after Celtic faced Inter Milan in the European Cup Final.

But before this extraordinary week for Scottish domestic football, Waddell covered Scotland's famous triumph over World Cup holders England at Wembley on 15 April 1967. In his preview to the match, in which the Scots were firm underdogs against Alf Ramsey's all-conquering side, Waddell predicted a Celtic player would hold the key to success. He wrote: 'Bobby Lennox, the wee, quiet, shy lad from Ayrshire is the player who can lead Scotland to victory on star-studded Wembley this afternoon. England are red-hot favourites but the World Championship crown does not fit firmly on their heads. And what better place to send it spinning than the very scene where the Jules Rimet Trophy was won.'

In his match report on Monday morning, the patriotic Waddell was clearly

Waddell didn't hesitate to criticize former managerial colleagues in his new media role.

Scotland's 1967 victory over England at Wembley brought triumphant praise from Waddell in the *Scottish Daily Express.*

jubilant at Scotland's amazing 3–2 triumph, a scoreline which flattered the well-beaten English. He thundered, 'England can keep their World Championship title. They're welcome to it. For Scotland have a new and more glamorous one – Out Of This World Champions. These were no ordinary mortals who whipped Sir Alf Ramsey's "boys" at Wembley, they were supermen. Scotland have had many wonderful victories on the sacred turf but none has matched the sheer soccer elegance which reduced England to ashes.'

The following month, Waddell was in the *Express*'s five-man party which travelled first to Lisbon for the European Cup Final and then on to Nuremberg for the Cup-Winners' Cup Final. In his preview to Celtic's historic showdown with Inter Milan, Waddell warned of the dangers presented by Helenio Herrera's Italian side but predicted glory for Jock Stein's men. He wrote: 'It will be tough but I take Celtic to bring the European Cup to Scotland, indeed Britain, for the first time.' Waddell was proved right of course and joined in the praise which was heaped upon the Parkhead men after their superb 2–1 win.

The pressure was now on Rangers to make it a Scottish double the following Wednesday. Waddell predicted they would do just that but, to his dismay, Scot Symon's side were beaten 1–0 by Bayern Munich in extra-time of a tense and disappointing match. 'Rangers, gallant though they were in this cauldron of more than 60,000 bawling, howling Germans,' wrote Waddell, 'lacked the vital spark in attack to win. Though they had most of the pressure throughout, they just did not have the inspiration to clinch the game.'

The *Express* coverage of the final didn't please Rangers who banned John Mackenzie from Ibrox for what they claimed was a personal attack on chairman John Lawrence. Unperturbed, the criticism only intensified in the follow-up articles on Friday 2 June. Waddell spared no-one at Ibrox as he looked at what the immediate future held for the club he unquestionably still held close to his heart. He wrote: 'Rangers face the day of reckoning – the day they must examine the cold hard facts. Bluntly, they are second rate compared with the successful outfits in Europe. Not one unit in the set-up can escape indictment. From the head of the house all the way down the line there has been a sad lack of ideas, of sheer professionalism in knowing what it takes to promote a top-ranking club. What a tragedy that the Rangers Football Club, who have always maintained themselves to be the best, should now be rated with the also-rans.'

Later that month, Rangers appointed Davie White as their assistant manager as they looked to respond to Stein's Celtic revolution. White had been manager of Clyde and was a forward-thinking coach who had travelled with both members of the Old Firm to their respective European finals in order to pick up more experience. Less than six months later, he would find himself taking over as manager of Rangers at the age of thirty-four when Scot Symon was sensationally sacked.

Rangers had made a decent enough start to the 1967–8 season. They had recovered from the disappointment of being knocked out of the League Cup by Celtic and were unbeaten at the top of the championship table after eight league games. But on Wednesday 1 November, the day Celtic were playing Racing Club in Argentina for the World Club Championship, Symon was dismissed and White was given his job. The Rangers board had given a knee-jerk reaction to jeers from the Ibrox fans during and after the 0–0 draw at home to Dunfermline the previous Saturday and gained little credit from the manner of Symon's dismissal, chairman Lawrence sending a third party to tell him the news.

The decision provoked widespread condemnation and prompted a stunned Waddell to write one of his most emotive pieces, about a man he had both played alongside and under at Ibrox. Under the headline 'Scot Symon The Great – Half his life a Ranger', Waddell wrote: 'About football I have never been a sentimentalist. But when I heard yesterday that Scot Symon was no longer the Rangers boss, I had to hold back the tears. For sadly the doors of Ibrox have closed for the last time on one of the great Rangers of all time.

'When they named him James Scotland Symon they could well have included the name Rangers. Almost half a lifetime Symon as player and manager has given to Rangers a greatness, a vital link in the long history of success that has made the club a legend.

'Scot Symon as player did not rate the aura of immortality of Meiklejohn or Morton or McPhail. Nor as manager was he accorded the esteem of Struth. But the Symon I know, the Symon I grew up with in football as player, as my boss and latterly as rival manager, in my book stands shoulder to shoulder with the all-time greats. The very history of Rangers has been written by men like Symon, who dedicated every minute of their day in a bid to further glorify the name of the club. Symon lived not for Symon – but for Rangers.

'Alas, now goes the last of the men who was schooled and developed in the strict school that made Rangers – the sense of loyalty, the strength of character, the name without a blemish, and the realization of the point that Mr Struth imprinted on every Rangers heart: the club is greater than any individual. These are the very factors which put Rangers on a pedestal every bit as much as the football skill of any player. As I watch Rangers now I stop to think how many have that deep sense of Symon feeling.

Scot Symon won six League championships, five Scottish Cups and four League Cups as Rangers manager and took the club to two European Finals.

37

'I was the first Rangers player to be introduced to Scot Symon when he joined the club. I was the first to greet him again on his return as manager. I had a great respect for him and it has not lessened over the years. As a player he was an inspiration by example. He had that Rangers quality of giving everything for victory and, of course, the opposite extreme of great personal failure in defeat. Symon is not the prima donna, who courts publicity in success. Rather he shuns the limelight, preferring to enjoy the peace and quiet of his home, satisfied in a job well done. And this was Symon the manager. He has never changed in that respect. Indeed, that is probably one of the reasons he has not been accorded the credit he was due.

'Symon has sat for almost fourteen years in the hottest seat in football. Sometimes securely, sometimes shakily. But always he has been unswerving in his loyalty. That Symon was a great Rangers manager there is no doubt. He took over control at a time when the great players of the latter days of Struth were on the wane. The transition proved the qualities of the man. I was there at Ibrox to watch the forming of a side which equalled any in their history. The days of Jimmy Millar and Ralph Brand could stand comparison with any before them. And I say that in all sincerity and honesty. I had played in great Rangers teams, but I put the eleven of Symon's early days far ahead of ours in sheer football skill and public entertainment.

'But regretfully Symon has been caught up in the soccer revolution of the past few years. Changes have come quickly. Desk managers are of the past. The men with drive and ambition are out in tracksuits. Symon could not change to that attitude. He is a lone wolf, an introvert. His troubles he keeps to himself. He carries the burden of defeat on his own shoulders. He takes the blame for mistakes and errors. The result is that he became closer and closer in himself, more conscious in these days of increased tension of the demands on the football manager.

'Symon has always accepted the fact that as manager of Rangers he was subject to intense criticism. His team decisions were severely torn apart, the wisdom of his planning was often in doubt. But what football manager's actions are not? Through it all, however, Scot Symon has maintained dignity and integrity, when it would have been so easy to throw mud and pass the buck along the line.

'Surely there is a place for James Scotland Symon at Ibrox? He has so much experience and character that a great club like Rangers could put to advantage. His record deserves better than peremptory dismissal.'

The following day, coach Bobby Seith resigned in the wake of Symon's axing to leave the relatively inexperienced Smith ploughing a lone furrow in charge. Waddell had no doubt Rangers were in crisis and wrote: 'The solid foundations of Rangers are rocking.

As a former Ranger, proud of the great tradition and wonderful reputation of the club, I am shaken. David White is on his own – the strain on the thirty-four year old has increased one hundred fold within a matter of hours.'

Despite all the controversy, White made an impressive start at Ibrox. The side won nineteen of their first twenty league games under his leadership, the only blemish a 2–2 draw with Celtic on 2 January 1968. In fact, White's side lost only one match in the championship all season, on the final day at home to Aberdeen – a result which allowed Celtic to lift their third successive title by two points.

White was trying to introduce a progressive style of play into the Rangers team and at times it worked well, notably in a 4–2 win over Celtic at Parkhead at the start of the 1968–9 season. But consistency, or the lack of it, stepped up the pressure on the young manager as the campaign failed to land a trophy. If semi-final defeat against Newcastle United in the Fairs Cup was painful, a 4–0 thrashing by Celtic in the Scottish Cup Final was quite simply a nightmare for White. He probably knew he had to land silverware in 1969–70, the season when Jim Baxter rejoined the club from Nottingham Forest in a bid to recapture former glories. But the gamble never really paid off as Rangers made a stuttering start to the campaign.

Waddell was in the press party which accompanied Rangers to Romania for the second leg of their European Cup-Winners' Cup first-round tie against Steaua Bucharest. Two Willie Johnston goals had earned a 2–0 win in the first leg and given Rangers plenty of confidence for the return in Bucharest on 1 October 1969. Waddell praised the defensive display of Davie White's team in the goalless draw at Ibrox and even comparing them with the famous 'Iron Curtain' rearguard of the Rangers side of his playing days.

But when Rangers lost 3–1 at home to Hibs in a league match ten days later, Waddell began to seriously question the direction the club were taking. In his match report he said, 'Did not chairman John Lawrence say two years ago in Nuremberg when they lost to Bayern Munich that Rangers would never again play with so many half-backs in the forward line? Well, here they were again in a vital match with half-backs Sandy Jardine and Bobby Watson listed in attack, even though they were playing in midfield.

'Manager Davie White has said in the past that he could not play Jim Baxter and Dave Smith in the same side because of their similarity in style. What of Jardine and Watson, both mere plodders, lacking in pace and constructive ability? They are hard enough tacklers...but surely that is not the criterion for a place in a Rangers side which expects to be top of the league.

'There must be some explanation, surely, for a team with personalities like Greig, McKinnon, Baxter, Henderson, Stein and Johnston, hitting such a rock-bottom performance as a team.'

Waddell was never short of an opinion and clearly didn't mind who he upset by expressing it. He also created a stir when he covered Scotland's qualifying campaign for the 1970 World Cup Finals which floundered on defeats in Germany and Austria.

Waddell suggested that the SFA should drop all of the English-based Scots for future games and claimed team boss Bobby Brown was not getting the best out of his players. He wrote: 'Forget the Anglos and build a team of home Scots. Be more demanding on the players who do wear Scotland jerseys. Get ruthless, Mr Brown!'

Ruthless was a word which certainly applied to Waddell, both as a manager and a journalist.

Little did he know it, but as he flew out with the Rangers party to Poland for the first leg of their Cup-Winners' Cup second round tie against Gornik Zabrze in November 1969, Waddell was approaching the end of his journalistic career. When Davie White announced his intention to attack on Polish soil to the press the day before the match, Waddell was less than impressed. In his preview in the *Express* on 12 November, he wrote: 'It is a bold gamble and a complete reversal of all the accepted tactics in European matches away from home when clubs normally concentrate almost entirely on defence. Surely this is a tremendous chance to take in a match that Davie White said last week would be "the toughest Rangers have had to face since I took over as manager".' Waddell added that Rangers were 'not equipped' for an attacking game.

His fears were confirmed as Rangers lost 3–1, although only an eighty-eighth-minute goal from the superb Lubanski denied White what would have been a creditable result away from home.

Two weeks later, Waddell was perched high up in the Ibrox press box to give his verdict on what proved to be the end of Davie White's managerial reign at Rangers. Jim Baxter's eighteenth-minute goal gave Rangers some hope of overturning the first-leg deficit but a superb second-half display by Gornik shattered the Ibrox players and supporters. Three goals in a sensational seventeen-minute spell repeated the first-leg win for the Poles and sent Rangers tumbling out of the tournament on a 6–2 aggregate.

Waddell was scathing in his match report, saying: 'Rangers suffered their final indignity at Ibrox last night. Poor Rangers are no nearer their dreams of success in Europe than ever they were. What can be said? Just the simple fact that Rangers are just not good enough. Another sad, sad night for Rangers. What now?'

What now was the sack for White. Around 3,000 fans had gathered outside the ground after the match demanding his departure but there was no hint the Rangers board would take that line. However, when White turned up at Ibrox the following morning, he was summoned to a board meeting at 10 am and dismissed.

In his most dramatic and certainly most famous article in the *Express*, Willie Waddell gave his verdict but with still no hint of the dramatic part he was to play in the immediate future for Rangers.

Under a banner back-page headline 'Why the boy David had to go', Waddell wrote: 'Davie White is the boy who tried to run an empire and failed ... because he just did not realize or appreciate all the implications, involvements and intricacies of being manager of the Rangers Football Club. And frankly it was no great surprise that his reign at Ibrox lasted a mere two years and twenty-six days.' Waddell also reproached White for getting involved in the very public slanging match with famous Glasgow comedian Lex McLean who had been making consistent jokes about Rangers. That, said Waddell, was 'not the done thing'.

Waddell went on to provide his assessment of what a Rangers manager should be, clearly drawing on his experiences under his biggest influence, Bill Struth. He wrote: 'The Rangers manager, by image, was someone apart from ordinary mortals – proud by nature, remote in character, respected by all, completely wrapped up in the image and good name of the club. A somewhat ghostly figure who commanded from his eyrie at the top of the marble stairs...who submerged himself in the

'Rangers were not travelling along the proper paths. Their image off the field was just as damaging as their results on it. Rangers were built on discipline and character.'

great tradition of the club. For in that word tradition lies the secret and power of Rangers.' He continued: 'Rangers were not travelling along the proper paths. Their image off the field was just as damaging as their results on it. Rangers were built on discipline and character. That had been sadly dented. Maybe Davie White was too modern, too liberal in his outlook.'

It was a remarkable piece which caught the imagination of Rangers fans who bombarded the *Express* with letters praising and agreeing with Waddell's sentiments. Even so, there was still no hint of Waddell making a dramatic return to Ibrox as manager, despite his topping an *Express* poll asking Rangers supporters who they wanted to succeed Davie White. The papers, *Express* included, speculated over Eddie Turnbull of Aberdeen or George Farm of Dunfermline being the Rangers board's choice.

On Monday 1 December, Waddell was at Parkhead to cover Celtic's 2–0 league win over St Mirren. The following night, he reported Kilmarnock's 4–1 victory against St Johnstone at Rugby Park. On Wednesday 3 December 1969 he penned his final article for the *Express* as it was announced he was to become the new manager of Rangers. Waddell signed off his journalistic career by giving the newspaper an exclusive insight into why he was returning to football. He revealed: 'Twice I had feelers from Rangers in the past and I was not interested but once a Ranger, always a Ranger. My driving force and ambition will be applied with the same amount of dedication and application.'

He admitted it would have been easy to continue his successful work as a football writer but pointed out, 'I am not a person who can lie back content in security.'

Willie Waddell was about to return to the other side of the interview room and would fill more column inches in the sports pages than ever before.

CHAPTER FIVE
BACK AT IBROX

At 4.52 PM ON WEDNESDAY 3 DECEMBER 1969 RANGERS MADE ONE OF THE MOST momentous announcements in their history. After two days of negotiations, Willie Waddell was installed as only the fifth manager since the club's foundation ninety-seven years earlier. Now forty-eight years old, Waddell handed in his notice as a sports writer for the *Scottish Daily Express* and walked back up the marble staircase at Ibrox as a Rangers employee. In many ways, the job was seen as something of a poisoned chalice. Rangers had not ruled since their last championship win in 1964 and their last major trophy success had been the Scottish Cup two years later.

The five-man Rangers board of chairman John Lawrence, Matt Taylor, Ian McLaren, George Brown and David Hope were considered by many to be more of a hindrance than a help to whoever was manager. Rumours of interference in team matters were rife and the sackings of White and Scot Symon before him, both controversial in their own way, only served to fuel that feeling among Ibrox followers.

'I did not believe I would ever come back into the game and, believe me, I would never have returned for any club but Rangers. I took two days to think it over before accepting. I have the conditions I wanted for the job. It is a tremendous job and it carries a great responsibility. The players must have pride in themselves, in their character and in their public image. The success of any club is founded off the field before a ball is kicked.'

Waddell had already turned down many offers, including attractive and lucrative ones from Manchester City, Wolves, Vancouver Whitecaps and Scotland to come out of managerial retirement. But when the call from Rangers came, with his old team-mate and friend Willie Thornton offering encouragement, Waddell was tempted. He clearly felt he could turn around the fortunes of the club he had served so magnificently and successfully as a player.

He made it plain he would only take the job on his terms. He had to have 100 per cent control of team affairs and would tolerate absolutely no interference from the board. When this was agreed, Waddell signed on for a reported salary of around £6,000 a year. He proved to be worth every penny for Rangers, even though he spent less than three years in the job.

As he was formally welcomed on the steps of Ibrox by chairman Lawrence, Waddell said, 'I did not believe I would ever come back into the game and, believe me, I would never have returned for any other club but Rangers. I took two days to think it over before accepting. I have the conditions I wanted for the job. It is a tremendous job and it carries a great responsibility. The players must

Welcomed back to Ibrox by Rangers chairman John Lawrence (above) and sat in the dug-out with Willie Thornton (below).

John Greig became Waddell's captain, confidant and link with the rest of the Rangers players.

have pride in themselves, in their character and in their public image. The success of any club is founded off the field before a ball is kicked.'

The appointment won widespread approval. Walter McCrae, who worked with Waddell at Kilmarnock and was one of his successors as Rugby Park boss, said, 'Willie Waddell is bound to be a success because of his positive thinking. He is thorough, efficient and vigorous.' The news of Waddell's return to Ibrox even produced a response south of the border where the decline of Rangers had been noted with interest. Harry Catterick, a leading English manager of the time with Everton, had got to know Waddell when the pair had met during one of the New York tournaments in which Kilmarnock and the Goodison club had both participated. 'Willie Waddell is a real competitor,' said Catterick, 'a man who will do anything within the rules to get his team winning. A man I will always admire.'

Waddell's reputation as a strict disciplinarian went before him and for some of the Rangers players it was a concern. Jim Baxter and Willie Henderson had been at the centre of the controversy in the build-up to the fateful Gornik tie which cost White his job, missing training at Largs one day when they overslept. Both men were eventually cleared of anything more than innocently missing their alarm call but they clearly felt the arrival of Waddell warranted a change in their appearance at the very least. In a high-profile act featured in the media, Baxter and Henderson visited a Glasgow barber to have their hair cropped and their moustaches shaved off!

Waddell, of course, was a disciple of Bill Struth's Ibrox era, a time when dress code and appearance were almost as important as performances on the pitch. He wasted absolutely no time in making his presence felt when he officially took up his new duties. Club captain John Greig, who would forge an unbreakable bond with Waddell, recalled Waddell's first day in the manager's chair, saying, 'I knew all about his reputation as a Rangers player and I knew him on a personal level as our paths had often crossed while I was on international duty with Scotland and he was working for the *Express*. We already had a good relationship and there was a mutual respect there before he even became Rangers manager.

'The first thing he did on his first day was to call me in to his office an hour before he met the rest of the players. Basically he told me he expected me to help him put his ideas across to the rest of the squad. He had been brought up on the Bill Struth style of discipline and tradition at the club and I'd worked under the same style with Scot Symon. Rangers were going through a really hard time and Willie intended to drag them up by the bootlaces which suited me fine. He demanded discipline and he went through anyone who stepped out of line like a dose of salts.'

Willie Johnston enjoyed a successful, if explosive relationship with Waddell.

Sandy Jardine had already been at Ibrox for four years prior to Waddell's arrival but it was under the new manager that his magnificent career for club and country took off. 'I owe him a lot,' says Jardine, who now works in the commercial department at Ibrox. 'Davie White had been thrown in at the deep end as Rangers manager after Scot Symon was sacked and, to be honest, the club had gone into decline. At the same time, Celtic were enjoying the greatest period of their history under Jock Stein so it really needed someone special to turn things around at Ibrox. It needed a strong character and that's what Willie was in every sense. He was a great believer in the Rangers traditions, he was steeped in them, and some of the standards he associated with the club had slipped badly. That was his first priority when he took over and any players who were not prepared to accept his code of discipline found themselves leaving the club.'

Winger Willie Johnston, a volatile character whose career married fabulous skill with consistent disciplinary problems, was one of those who might have expected to fall foul of the new regime. Instead, the little Fifer found himself enjoying a profitable love-hate

Colin Stein's goals played a major role in Waddell's success story as Rangers manager.

relationship with Waddell from day one. 'I remember his first day clearly,' recalls Johnston, now a publican in Kirkcaldy. 'I was worried about his appointment, a lot of the lads were, because he had been slaughtering us in his column in the *Express*. We were all in the dressing room that morning when he marched in and slammed the door shut behind him. He just said, "My name's Waddell, some of you already know me and those of you who don't soon will."'

'He was a ruthless guy but as it turned out I got on brilliantly with him and he got the best out of me as a player. Sure, we argued like cat and dog and I think I was up and down the marble stairs to his office more than any other player. He always had the last word, his decision was final but the great thing was he never held a grudge against you. He rescued Rangers at that time, there's no doubt about it, because the club was going downhill fast.'

'For his first few days, he got the tracksuit back on and came out to the Albion training ground and worked among the players,' adds Greig. 'But he looked so out of place with a tracksuit on, it wasn't his style, and I think he realized that quickly. He then took to just standing at the side of the training pitch watching us and leaving the coaching staff to get on with it. But everyone knew who was the boss. He always believed in being together, being a unit. He had a good idea of the game and used to pick the right team for a specific job.'

Waddell's first game in charge was against Hearts at Tynecastle in the league on Saturday 6 December 1969. He must have wondered what he had taken on when the Edinburgh men opened the scoring after just forty seconds. But his new charges recovered and goals from Colin Stein and Johnston – how the names of those scorers would figure in Waddell's reign – gave Rangers a 2–1 win.

Four more league wins followed and a goalless draw with Celtic at an icy Parkhead as the 1970s were ushered in installed Rangers as genuine title contenders. But the team had flattered to deceive and a 2–1 defeat by Raith Rovers signalled the end of the run and Rangers slithered their way to the end of the campaign as Celtic lifted their fifth consecutive crown with twelve points to spare.

The summer of 1970 would be one of change as Waddell set about moulding Rangers in his own image. Sentiment had no part to play as he took the tough decision to axe his former team-mate Davie Kinnear from the backroom staff after twenty-six years of service. Harold Davis and Laurie Smith also moved out as Waddell assembled his own coaching team. Jock Wallace was recruited from Hearts, having already forged a reputation as one of

'We were all in the dressing room that morning when he marched in and slammed the door shut behind him. He just said, "My name's Waddell, some of you already know me and those of you who don't soon will."'

the most uncompromising trainers in Scottish football. In effect, Wallace was Waddell's number two although Willie Thornton, who had been acting manager on White's dismissal retained the title of assistant manager and remained his most trusted lieutenant. Wallace's appointment would prove to be inspired, although he had not actually been Waddell's first choice. He had tried to take Walter McCrae from Kilmarnock and was none too pleased when his former assistant at Kilmarnock, now boss at Rugby Park, turned him down. McCrae later recalled, 'We were a good team, Willie and I, but I refused to go to Rangers. Willie was furious at my refusal. He wasn't used to being refused at that time but I was too much of a Kilmarnock man to leave.'

Waddell had also identified individual areas of improvement which were required by certain players, as Johnston and Jardine recall. He was a great believer in sprinting and he sent Sandy and I to take part in Highland Games races that summer,' says Johnston. 'It made a big difference to my game. I preferred to play as an inside-forward but he wanted me at outside-left or outside-right. 'He was a great help to me, he passed on things having been a winger himself.'

Jardine also felt the benefit of the extra sprint training. He says, 'I eventually won a professional 100-yard race at one of the meetings. Pace was very important as far as he was concerned, maybe because he was a real flier as a player himself by all accounts.

'It was pretty much this season or bust for me when Willie Waddell took over as manager. We were already out of the league race so he used a lot of the games to experiment. I played left-back at first then he moved me to right-back. I did reasonably well there and basically he kept me there permanently after that. You can't say one person made your career successful but his decision to put me to right-back certainly helped me become a success with Rangers and Scotland.

'Waddell's strength basically was that he was a bully. He picked the right people to play in the right situations and managed to get them to do what they were told. I wouldn't say he was a tactical manager. He just knew what he wanted and if you didn't come up to his standards, you didn't get a second chance.

'He relished an argument but he never held a grudge. If someone stepped out of line, he could be really harsh but the next day it was forgotten about. If you did the business for him on the park, he would look after you. He didn't just make me a better player, he taught me to be a better person too.'

Waddell's only major signing in his first few months was goalkeeper Peter McCloy who was recruited from Motherwell. But out went a host of established

Peter McCloy was Waddell's first major signing when he arrived from Motherwell in a swap deal which took Bobby Watson and Brian Heron to Fir Park.

names, including the iconic figure of Baxter whose off-field excesses brought his career to a premature end.

McCloy, who went on to make more appearances for Rangers than any other keeper in the club's history, sensed he was in on the start of something big. 'Everyone knew what Waddell had achieved at Kilmarnock,' recalls McCloy, 'and it was generally felt he could turn Rangers around. I had come across him when he was with the *Express* and he came to Fir Park one day as part of a series he was writing on all the clubs in Scotland. He had a wide knowledge of all the players in the country which probably gave him a head start when he agreed to go back into football and take the Ibrox job.

'I was part-time at Motherwell and I remember being pulled aside at training on a Thursday night to be told I was to get myself along to Ibrox the next day. It was actually Friday the thirteenth but it was one of the luckiest days of my career. It didn't take long to sort things out. That was one thing about Willie Waddell as a manager, he didn't negotiate, he just told you what you were getting! In those days, it was an honour to get up the stairs to his office.

'He was a real disciplinarian and one of the first things you were told when you signed was that you must adhere to a strict dress code. But one thing which came across quickly to me was that he was incredibly loyal to his players. He might give you the biggest row imaginable behind closed doors but he would defend you to the hilt in public. That meant his players were loyal to him and I think that played a major part in the success Waddell achieved as Rangers manager.

'Bringing Jock Wallace in was a big step. He let Jock run the coaching side of things but Waddell was always there, standing at the side of the pitch, saying nothing but watching everything that was going on.'

The Waddell-Wallace partnership quickly found favour with the Rangers players, despite the unprecedented demands of the new training regime they introduced. 'Jock took the training and Waddell did the tactics,' says Johnston. 'They were a good team. One would bawl and shout at you, one would take you aside and whisper encouragement in your ear.'

Jardine concurs: 'He and Jock were a good pairing. The training demands increased, it was physically very hard. If you look at that team, so many of us continued playing well into our thirties and that was no coincidence. It was down to the fitness regime of Waddell and Wallace.'

Waddell took Rangers to Germany to prepare for his first full season in charge, a season which would see him end the club's trophy famine. Tragically, the 1970–71 season was completely overshadowed by the Ibrox Disaster which saw sixty-six people die after the New Year Old Firm match. (Waddell's admirable and indefatigable reaction to the calamitous event is detailed in Chapter Seven.)

Rangers made a reasonable start to the campaign, coasting through their League Cup qualifying section and winning five of their first eight games in the championship. Their only defeat in that period was a 2–0 loss to Celtic at

Parkhead which starkly illustrated just how far behind Stein's side they still were.

Waddell's first tilt at European glory with Rangers saw them given the toughest possible draw when they were paired with Bayern Munich in the first round of the Fairs Cup. The first leg was in Bayern's Grunwald Stadium and Rangers should have emerged with a far better outcome than what was a creditable 1–0 defeat. They created several chances against the Bavarian side but Greig's bullet header against the crossbar was the closest they came to beating Sepp Maier in the home goal. It took a piece of brilliance from the peerless Franz Beckenbauer to give Bayern a priceless advantage to take to Glasgow. The German genius strolled forward from his own half and played a one-two with Paul Breitner before giving McCloy no chance with a low twenty-yard shot.

There were over 80,000 at Ibrox a fortnight later to see if Rangers could turn the tie around. The second leg hinged on a moment of controversy ten minutes from time with the score at 0–0. Bayern were awarded a free-kick on the edge of the Rangers penalty area and the Swiss referee held his arm aloft to indicate it was indirect. Gerd Muller then stepped up and swerved the ball beyond McCloy and into the net via the inside of a post. McCloy recalls, 'I couldn't believe it, because the ref had clearly signalled for an indirect free-kick. I calmly picked the ball out of the net and placed it for a goal-kick but the next thing I knew the ref had given a goal and their players were celebrating. It was a crazy decision and as it came so late in the game, it gave us no chance of coming back.'

As it turned out, Stein equalized for Rangers a minute later and in a frantic closing period they were denied another by the brilliance of Maier. Bayern went through 2–1 on aggregate but Waddell and Rangers had learned a valuable European lesson which would be put to good use the following season.

On the domestic front, Rangers looked for compensation and it came in the shape of the League Cup. Hibs were stylishly swept aside 6–2 on aggregate in the quarter-finals to set up a Hampden semi-final with surprise package Cowdenbeath. Goals from Johnston and Stein secured the passage to the final far more convincingly than the 2–0 scoreline suggested. Not unexpectedly, Celtic stood in the way of Waddell delivering to Rangers their first trophy in over four years. The Parkhead men had surprisingly needed a replay to beat Dumbarton in the other semi-final but they were nonetheless odds-on favourites to lift the League Cup for the sixth successive year.

The portents were not good for Waddell going into the final at a wet Hampden

Derek Johnstone leaps between Billy McNeill and Jim Craig to give Waddell his first trophy as Rangers manager with the only goal of the 1970 League Cup Final against Celtic.

on 24 October 1970. His team had been humbled 2–0 by Aberdeen at Ibrox in the league the previous Saturday, an example of the inconsistency which would plague their title challenge. To make matters worse, skipper Greig was ruled out of the final by a bout of 'flu. Waddell, always a promoter of young talent, then took a decision which stunned everyone but proved inspired. Derek Johnstone, a precocious sixteen year old, had scored twice on his first-team debut the previous month, a 5–0 league stroll against Cowdenbeath at Ibrox. He had not featured again since and seemed to be a player Waddell was keeping for the future. But the Rangers manager decided Johnstone could be his trump card and named him as his number nine to face Celtic. Johnstone, who went on to have an outstanding career for Rangers, had never even been to Hampden to watch a match before but now he found himself facing a Celtic side full of stars who had won the European Cup just three years before.

His selection came as a surprise to the rest of the Rangers players, as Sandy Jardine recalls. 'At the time it was a brave decision,' said Jardine, 'and although we all knew Derek was going to be a quality player, no-one expected him to be in the frame for the final.'

It was fairy-tale stuff simply to be chosen to play in such a match at his tender age but Johnstone turned it into the ultimate boy's own story. Five minutes from the end of a first half Rangers were starting to control came a moment Johnstone will never forget and which sparked the Willie Waddell success story as Rangers manager. Willie Henderson and Alex MacDonald combined to set Willie Johnston scampering down the right. The winger swung over a perfect cross aimed for Johnstone but the teenage striker was third favourite to reach it as he leaped between two of Celtic's Lisbon Lions, skipper Billy McNeill and Jim Craig. But it was Johnstone who

The teeenage Johnstone is joined by Colin Jackson and Alex MacDonald as Rangers celebrate their first trophy for four years.

timed his jump to perfection, as he would do many more times in a Rangers jersey, and he planted a magnificent header beyond stunned Celtic goalkeeper Evan Williams. In front of 106,263 fans, the sixteen year old had scored what proved to be the only goal of the final.

Johnstone later recalled Waddell's words to the Rangers players at half-time. He had told them, 'Celtic are the champions and you're maybe going to have to defend here but if you keep your nerve you should get the result you want.'

Waddell's players did hold their nerve and to the joy of the long-suffering Rangers fans, stand-in captain Ronnie McKinnon climbed the Hampden steps to collect the League Cup. 'It was a fabulous and emotional day for the club,' recalls Jardine, one of the heroes. 'They say you always remember your first time and I've certainly never forgotten that match. I'd played in the Cup-Winners' Cup Final in 1967, when we lost to Bayern Munich in extra-time, but this was my first winner's medal. We played really well on the day and deserved to win, no question.

'That was the start for Rangers under Willie Waddell. He had broken the mould and that laid the foundations for us to take over from Celtic as the dominant force in the 1970s.'

Waddell savoured the achievement but knew his rebuilding of Rangers had only just started, a fact underlined by their League form. Rangers won just three of their eight Leagues games immediately after the League Cup triumph and gradually slipped out of title contention. However, the Scottish Cup offered the chance to end the campaign on a high note with another trophy. Early rounds against Falkirk and St Mirren were safely negotiated and Aberdeen were edged out 1–0 in a tense quarter-final at Ibrox. After a goalless draw, Rangers beat Hibs 2–1 in a pulsating semi-final replay with Alfie Conn notching the winner. Two nights later, Celtic set up another Old Firm final showdown when they beat Airdrie in their replay.

Remarkably, Waddell again included Johnstone in his plans, this time as substitute. With Rangers trailing to a Bobby Lennox goal in front of 120,092 at Hampden, on 8 May 1971, the teenager was sent on in place of Andy Penman with twenty minutes remaining. Three minutes from time, Johnstone proved his League Cup Final goal was no fluke as he leapt to head a dramatic equalizer beyond Williams.

Waddell sprang another selection surprise in the replay four days later, handing previously unknown twenty-one year old Jim Denny his first-team debut. Denny responded well to the challenge but two goals in as many minutes from Lou Macari and Harry Hood put Celtic 2–0 up at the interval. A Jim Craig own goal in the second half gave Rangers hope but this time not even substitute Johnstone could save the day. Nonetheless, Waddell's first full season had to be viewed as a success, as he had brought silverware to the club again.

Now he had to build on the League Cup success. No-one at Ibrox could even dream just how spectacular a renovation job it would prove to be.

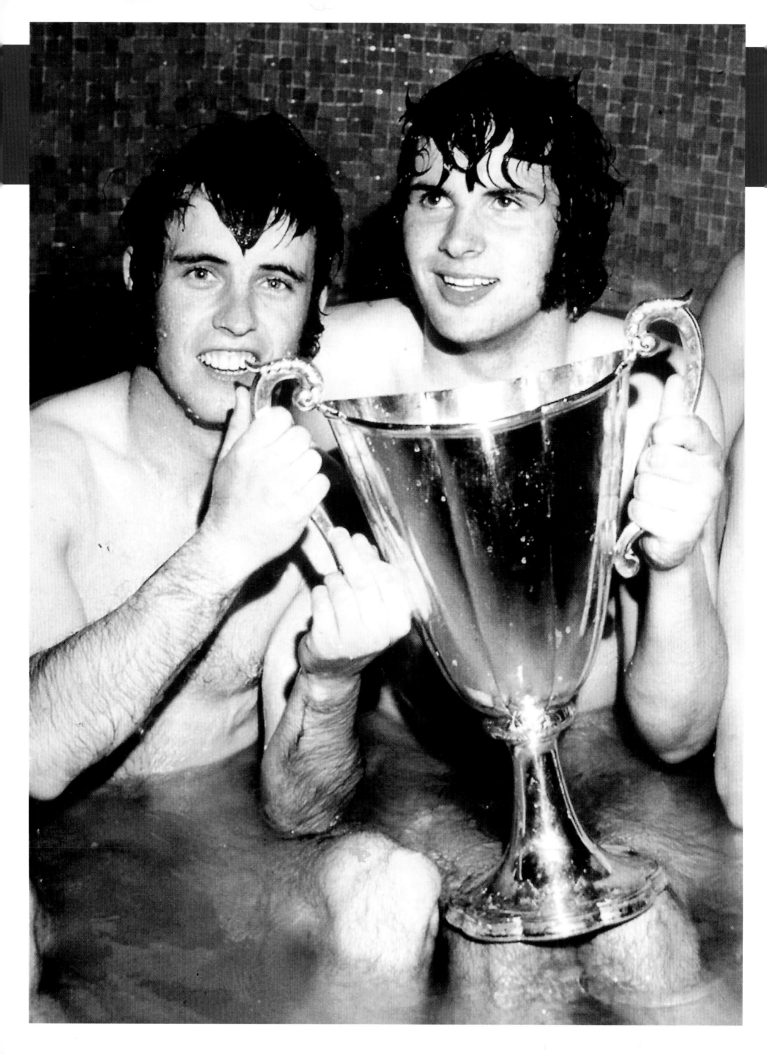

CHAPTER SIX
WADDELL'S FINEST HOUR

THE ROAD TO IMMORTALITY FOR WILLIE WADDELL AND HIS RANGERS PLAYERS BEGAN IN Gothenburg and ended in Barcelona. There were twists and turns aplenty along the way but the final destination in 1971–2 brought the Ibrox club the European trophy they so desperately craved.

Waddell took his squad to Sweden to prepare for the season. In the party was his one close-season signing, Tommy McLean – how shrewd an investment the £60,000 paid to Kilmarnock would prove to be. Waddell know McLean well from their time together at Rugby Park. The Rangers manager was always keen to have wingers in his squad and there were few better at the time than McLean whose pinpoint accuracy in delivering crosses would prove to be a vital weapon. Tottenham were also keen on the Killie star but Waddell's presence at Ibrox ensured McLean would choose Rangers ahead of the big-spending London outfit.

'He loved wingers, he had a real soft spot for them,' recalls Peter McCloy, 'obviously because he had been one himself. Wee Tommy was certainly one of the best.'

> **'He loved wingers, he had a real soft spot for them, obviously because he had been one himself. Wee Tommy was certainly one of the best.'**

The three-match pre-season trip to Gothenburg brought two victories and one defeat against Swedish opposition and allowed Waddell and Jock Wallace to formulate their strategy for a campaign in which they hoped to end Celtic's grip on the league championship.

When English First Division clubs Everton and Spurs were both beaten at Ibrox on their return from Sweden, optimism was running high in the dressing room and on the terraces. But that feelgood factor was quickly punctured when the competitive action got underway with the League Cup. The opening match of the qualifying section, against Celtic, took place at Ibrox, but was officially an away tie because Parkhead was undergoing reconstruction.

Jock Stein's men still managed to look far more at home than Rangers and gave Waddell plenty to think about as they recorded a 2–0 win which didn't flatter them. Goals from the inspired Jimmy Johnstone and a young Old Firm debutant by the name of Kenny Dalglish sunk Rangers who had little to offer in front of 72,500 fans.

Three straight wins over Ayr United (twice) and Morton kept Rangers in contention as they faced up to Celtic in the Ibrox 'return' two weeks later. But this time they were handed an even harsher lesson, the precocious Dalglish netting again as Celtic cruised to a 3–0 win and sent holders Rangers tumbling out of the League Cup.

Tommy McLean, an inspirational signing, celebrates Cup-Winners' Cup success in Barcelona with Derek Johnstone.

Attention now turned to the league championship but Rangers could hardly have made a worse start. On the opening day of the title race, they found themselves 3–1 down at half-time to Partick Thistle at Firhill and a second-half rally brought only a Colin Stein goal.

Rangers then had to face Celtic again on Saturday 11 September at Ibrox knowing victory was crucial if their league championship challenge was not to suffer a grievous early blow. The match also came just four days before they were to begin their European Cup-Winners' Cup campaign against Rennes in France. This time, Rangers performed far better but still lost. Lou Macari gave Celtic an early lead but Waddell's men stormed back and goals from Johnston and Stein put them 2–1 up at half-time. In a pulsating contest, Dalglish maintained his perfect scoring record in Old Firm matches to draw Celtic level. Rangers pressed for the winner and thought they had got it when Colin Stein lobbed Evan Williams. To the home team's dismay, referee John Paterson disallowed the goal for dangerous play by Stein. The official later admitted he had got it wrong after viewing television pictures but that was of no consolation to Rangers who were beaten by a Jimmy Johnstone goal a minute from time.

It was hardly the best preparation for a tough first-round European tie as Peter McCloy recalls. 'We started the season very poorly and no one gave us much of a chance going to France,' he says. 'Rennes were a useful team and we were hardly brimming with confidence. But as he did all through the season in Europe, Willie Waddell did his homework well and we got a great boost from how we played in France that night.'

'We started the season very poorly and no one gave us much of a chance going to France. Rennes were a useful team and we were hardly brimming with confidence.'

Waddell had been to Brittany to see Rennes beat Bastia 1–0 in a French League game a few weeks earlier. Rennes played well and their victory would have been far more convincing but for an inspired display from Bastia's Yugoslavian international keeper Ilya Pantelic. But of more concern to Waddell were two of Pantelic's countrymen who had just been signed by Rennes. Midfielder Kobechek and striker Mojsov were both Yugoslav internationals and, to Waddell's surprise, Rennes manager Jean Prouff claimed they would both be in the side to face Rangers. The Ibrox boss suspected neither had signed in time to play in the tie and checked it out with UEFA on his return to Glasgow. After protracted talks, the European governing body told Rennes they could field Mojsov but not Kobechek. Rennes coach Prouff took it badly and there was a fair amount of needle surrounding the tie when Rangers stepped onto the Parc des Sports on Wednesday 15 September.

Prouff was an astute and experienced coach and he already knew all about facing Rangers in Europe. He had been coach of Standard Liege when the Belgian side knocked Rangers out of the European Cup 4–3 on aggregate in the quarter-finals ten years earlier. He had also been at Ibrox on the Saturday to see Rangers edged out by Celtic and he combined diplomacy with mind games when confronted by the Scottish press afterwards. He said the power of Rangers concerned him and that his players would need to be at their best to advance in the tournament. Once back in France, however, Prouff was a confident man and with good reason. Rennes, with the midfield pair of Raymond Keruzore – compared to Jim Baxter by Waddell – and French international Andre Betta pulling the strings were riding high in the French League. Rangers, on the other hand, arrived in Brittany pointless and on the back of one of their worst starts to a domestic season.

Waddell, against his natural instincts, decided to play a containing game in a bid to set up the tie for victory in the second leg at Ibrox, handing the combative Alex MacDonald and skipper John Greig marking jobs on Keruzore and Betta. Rennes grew increasingly frustrated as the match wore on while Rangers started to look dangerous on the break. It was the Scots who finally made the crucial breakthrough, Willie Johnston showing tremendous composure to beat Rennes keeper Marcel Auboir.

It might have been even better for Rangers as McLean missed a decent chance to make it 2–0 as the French team committed everything to attack. In the end, Waddell had to settle for a 1–1 draw as Rennes substitute Redon finally found a way past McCloy twelve minutes from time.

The Rangers boss was a happy man though, but his French counterpart was quite the opposite. Prouff launched an astonishing blast at Rangers which only served to stoke the fires for the second leg at Ibrox. The Rennes boss fumed, 'That was not football Rangers played tonight. That was not the game of football as I know it or as my players know it or as our supporters know it. What the Scottish players did tonight had nothing to do with football. It was anti-football. They came here only to stop us playing instead of trying to play themselves. All Brittany is angry at the way this game was played.

'We will come to Glasgow in two weeks and when we are there we will show how football should be played. We believe that skill is more important than results. Winning a European tie is not as important to me as playing attractive football.'

Waddell was totally unmoved by his opposite number's outburst and, on the contrary, took a great deal of satisfaction from it. His tactics, which had gone so close to getting Rangers a draw in Munich the previous season, had worked. Waddell was streetwise in European football terms and Prouff probably realized it as much as anyone. The smiling Waddell said, 'If he (Prouff) comes to Ibrox to show us how to play then he will have to go some. We are in the commanding position in this tie and we intend to stay that way.'

Rangers duly took a lift from their display in France and on their return to domestic duty they finally got off the mark in the championship with a convincing 3–0 win over Falkirk at Brockville. Instead of lift-off, however, Rangers spluttered badly again in their next game as they lost 2–0 at home to Aberdeen.

John Greig exchanges pennants with Rennes skipper Cardiet before the match at Ibrox.

That was enough to prompt Monsieur Prouff to start making more bombastic noises when he arrived in Glasgow with his Rennes players for the second leg. 'Rangers lost to Aberdeen on Saturday so the problems for this game clearly lie with them,' Prouff told a press conference. 'We will win this game because my players have more skill than Rangers who rely only on power. No matter what happens in the game Rennes will remain a credit to football as always.'

Waddell refused to be drawn into a war of words and instead let his team do his talking for him on the pitch. There were 42,000 at Ibrox for a match Rangers controlled from start to finish. Rangers closed the door at the back and stretched Rennes in the wide areas at every opportunity. Waddell had recalled veteran wing man Willie Henderson at outside-right for his first match of the campaign and, along with Willie Johnston on the opposite flank, he forced the French onto the back foot for most of the contest.

The only surprise on the night was that Rangers did not win by more than 1–0. The solitary strike came in the thirty-eighth minute when Auboir failed to hold a shot from Johnston and MacDonald pounced to fire in the rebound. Auboir defied Rangers with several outstanding saves and was rescued by the woodwork when Colin Stein's header beat him.

Rangers were worthy winners and even Jean Prouff had to admit it. 'Rangers

Colin Stein rises above the French defence to flash a header just off target.

were the better team and deserved to win,' conceded the humbled Rennes coach. 'They showed more class and skill tonight, especially on the wings where Henderson and Johnston were outstanding.'

It was a hugely significant win for Rangers at a time when they needed it badly. Waddell was as relieved as he was delighted. 'We had to get a result in that game,' said the Rangers manager the following day. 'It was vital to stay in Europe and at the same time give us a boost for the league here at home. I was very pleased indeed with the way the players approached this match. They worked hard in both games and in each one we got the result we wanted.'

The second-round draw two days later handed Rangers an even tougher assignment, against Portuguese giants Sporting Lisbon. Back on the home front, Rangers suffered an immediate hangover when they lost 2–1 to Hearts at Tynecastle but they then gave themselves the boost Waddell had anticipated. In the two league matches prior to the first leg against Sporting, full points were collected with a 3–0 home win over East Fife and a 5–1 demolition of Dundee United at Tannadice.

Rangers ran out in front of 50,000 at Ibrox on Wednesday 20 October full of confidence and ready for the challenge presented by the star-studded Lisbon side.

Waddell had identified a possible weakness in Sporting's goalkeeper, Damas, who had played for Portugal in their 2–1 defeat against Scotland at Hampden the previous week. In a magnificent opening half-hour of sustained, powerful, attacking football Rangers exploited Damas to a degree even Waddell could not have anticipated. Rangers took the lead after just nine minutes when the keeper failed to deal with an Andy Penman free-kick and Colin Stein headed into the empty net. Waddell was forced to make a change shortly afterwards when Penman was injured so Alfie Conn came on and Rangers continued to dominate.

Ten minutes after his opener, Stein made it 2–0 thanks to some more erratic goalkeeping by Damas. This time the Sporting number one was caught in no-man's land by a Dave Smith free-kick and Colin Stein gratefully finished off from close range.

The Portuguese were reeling and in the twenty-eighth minute Rangers grabbed a third. Conn and Henderson deceived the defence with a well-worked free-kick and Henderson cut

Stein is on target this time as he nods the ball past Sporting Lisbon keeper Damas at Ibrox.

in from the right to smack an unstoppable shot beyond the hapless Damas. The tie appeared as good as over and rampant Rangers were unfortunate not to increase their lead further before half-time.

It was always going to be difficult for Rangers to maintain that level of performance in the second half and a three-goal lead was more than acceptable to take to Lisbon. But Rangers dropped their guard in the later stages and handed Sporting a lifeline which was gratefully accepted. Brazilian forward Chico pulled one back in the seventieth minute and the Portuguese side took heart. They finished the stronger and four minutes from time placed the tie back on a knife edge when substitute Pedro Gomes reduced the deficit to just 3–2. A night which had started so impressively for Rangers ended with the Scots in a precarious position for the second leg and Waddell knew it. 'We should have been five goals ahead at half-time,' he said, 'but we can still reach the quarter-finals.'

Damas is beaten by Stein again as Rangers make a superb start to the second round, first leg clash.

Sporting coach Fernando Vaz wore the look of a man given a last-minute pardon at the gallows. 'We should be out of the tournament after the way Rangers played in the first half,' he said, 'because they were magnificent. But we are back to life and we need just one more goal in Lisbon to get through. I am sure we will do it.'

Rangers posted another couple of heartening league displays before the return. Motherwell and Kilmarnock were both swept aside at Ibrox, 4–0 and 3–1 respectively, and although they remained seven points behind leaders Celtic in the championship table, confidence was now high.

They certainly needed all of their resilience as their journey out to Lisbon for the second leg turned into a nightmare. An air traffic control strike delayed Rangers' initial flight from Glasgow to London on the morning of Monday 1 November for several hours and saw them miss their scheduled flight to Portugal. Waddell and his players had to re-route from Heathrow to Stansted where the Rangers manager finally secured the services of a charter flight. The air traffic control dispute meant the charter was postponed until the Tuesday morning, forcing the weary Rangers party to hastily find hotel accommodation in the capital for the night. They eventually arrived at their Estoril base on the outskirts of Lisbon just three hours ahead of the twenty-four-hour limit prior to kick-off imposed by UEFA.

There were 60,000 inside the cavernous Jose Alvalade Stadium late on Wednesday night for one of the most remarkable European ties witnessed anywhere. Argentinian striker Hector Yazalde had been successfully contained by

Rangers in the first leg at Ibrox but he was pinpointed by Waddell as the danger man in Lisbon. His warning rang true when Yazalde put Sporting in front on the night in the twenty-fifth minute. 'It came from a free-kick and I felt I should have done better with it,' recalls McCloy.

It was 1–0 to Sporting, 3–3 on aggregate, a scoreline that would have been enough to take the Portuguese side through on away goals. The drama, however, had only just begun as two minutes later, Colin Stein levelled for Rangers and restored their slender overall advantage.

It was a wholly untypical European tie. Waddell's men tried to break forward at every opportunity to cancel out the away goals Sporting scored at Ibrox and it was end-to-end stuff. Eight minutes from half-time, midfielder Tome joined the attack and beat McCloy to put the home side 2–1 ahead. It was 4–4 on aggregate now with Sporting once more in the driving seat. Just a minute after the restart, the invaluable Colin Stein beat Damas again to make it 2–2 on the night and 5–4 on aggregate in Rangers' favour. The Ibrox men now seemed in control but suffered a terrible blow eighteen minutes from time when Ronnie McKinnon, having a magnificent match in central defence, suffered a double fracture of his right leg when he was recklessly challenged. McKinnon was stretchered off and taken to hospital and Dave Smith came on to join Colin Jackson at the back.

It seemed as if Rangers had held out when up popped Gomes to score for Sporting six minutes from the end. The teams were now level at 5–5 over the two legs and went into a nerve-shredding period of extra-time. Rangers looked the likelier side in the additional period and fully deserved Willie Henderson's terrific strike in the 100th minute of the contest. That was 3–3 on the night, 6–5 to Rangers on aggregate but, most significantly, they had now scored more away goals than Sporting. The home side now needed to score twice to win the tie. They barely deserved to score once but four minutes after Henderson's goal, a handball by Jackson gave Sporting a penalty which Perez converted. The second period of extra-time was goalless and at the final whistle, the Rangers players started to celebrate an away goals success after the 6–6 aggregate final score.

But, as keeper McCloy recounts clearly, Dutch referee Laurens Van Raavens had other ideas. 'I can remember Colin Stein and I jumping into each other's arms, leaping around and celebrating the fact we were into the quarter-finals,' says McCloy. 'But the next thing we knew, the ref was telling us away goals in extra-time did not count double and that the match would be decided on penalties. We couldn't believe it and after thinking we had won the tie, we had to get ourselves mentally ready for a shoot-out.'

Perhaps not surprisingly in the circumstances, the spot kicks were a nightmare for Rangers. They missed every one, Dave Smith even failing to score after the ref ordered his to be retaken. Sporting, on the other hand, kept their nerve and won the shoot-out 3–0. There were remarkable scenes as the Lisbon players were hoisted onto the shoulders of their delirious fans and began to celebrate victory. The crestfallen Rangers players trooped back to their dressing

In the penalty shoot-out that should not have taken place, Stein's effort is saved by Damas.

room in the belief their European dream was over for another year. Just as Waddell prepared to commiserate with them and try and lift their spirits, he was interrupted by John Fairgrieve, one of the Scottish journalists covering the match. The travelling media were convinced the Dutch official had got it wrong, that away goals in extra-time did count double and that the penalty shoot-out should not have taken place.

Waddell immediately sought out the UEFA observer for the match to point out Mr Van Raavens' blunder. The jubilant Rangers boss eventually returned to his players to tell them they would be in the quarter-final draw later that week. The official word that Rangers had in fact won the tie came in the early hours of the morning from UEFA general secretary Hans Bangerter. He said: 'Rangers have won. The referee is completely in error. It used to be that away goals did not count double during extra-time but that rule was changed and the referee should have known that.' The shell-shocked Sporting Lisbon directors launched a protest with UEFA the following day but it was in vain.

As Waddell reflected on a night of unprecedented drama, he said, 'I couldn't have been more proud of the way these lads worked out there in that match. If they had lost that game then it would have been one of the greatest injustices in European football.'

Rangers had now come through two enormously testing ties against clubs from countries with the highest football pedigree in France and Portugal. Any hope that life might get a little easier in the quarter-finals was squashed when the draw paired them with Italian high fliers Torino but that was four months away and in

'I couldn't have been more proud of the way these lads worked out there in that match. If they had lost that game then it would have been one of the greatest injustices in European football.'

the meantime Rangers looked to drag themselves back into contention for domestic glory.

There was no sign of weariness on their return from the Lisbon epic as they crushed St Johnstone 4–1 at Muirton Park the following Saturday. Waddell was dismayed when Rangers slipped up at Ibrox in their next match, losing 3–2 to Dundee, and laid it on the line to his players that a greater level of consistency was required. The response was a run of seven consecutive league wins, last-minute goals from Stein and Johnstone respectively clinching the last two against Hibs on Christmas Day and Partick Thistle on New Year's Day. Rangers had now hoisted themselves to third place in the table after such a miserable start to the campaign.

It meant the 3 January showdown with leaders Celtic at Parkhead offered them a chance to reassert themselves as serious title contenders. But for the fourth time that season, it was a dose of Old Firm misery for Waddell and his players. Jimmy Johnstone gave Celtic a 1–0 interval lead which was harsh on Rangers who had given as good as they had received. A point was the least they deserved and they looked to have secured it when Stein forced a Willie Mathieson pass beyond Denis Connaghan nine minutes from time. Celtic, though, had other ideas and an injury-time winner from Jim Brogan effectively ended Rangers' championship challenge. Their league form was a mixed bag after that, ranging from a scintillating display to hammer Hearts 6–0 at Ibrox to an abject 2–0 defeat at the hands of Motherwell at Fir Park.

Knock-out football offered Rangers their only hope of success now and they began their Scottish Cup campaign well enough. Falkirk were their first victims, 2–0 at Ibrox after a draw at Brockville, and then St Mirren were well beaten 4–1 at Love Street. But all Ibrox eyes were now firmly fixed on Europe and the Cup-Winners' Cup quarter-final against Torino. Rangers had to travel to Italy for the first leg in early March and gave themselves the ideal send-off with a 2–1 league win at Kilmarnock on the Saturday. There was an early celebration for Waddell with a champagne party in Turin to mark his fifty-first birthday on Tuesday 7 March just twenty-four hours before the match.

Rangers were firmly cast in the role of underdogs against a gifted Torino side who were challenging for the Serie A title. As McCloy remembers, it was the first time the manager made it clear he genuinely felt Rangers could win the Cup-Winners' Cup. 'Torino were top of the Italian League at the time and he got us together the day before the game over there for a long talk,' says McCloy. 'He said this was the game, that if we got past Torino we could win the trophy. It was the first time he had mentioned it. He said we could put ourselves in the history books. All of the boys left that meeting knowing what it was all about.'

Waddell knew his team needed a performance of discipline and steel in the vast bowl of the Stadio Comunale to keep the tie alive for the second leg. The broken leg that McKinnon had suffered in the previous round had been a huge blow. But Waddell had successfully recast his defence by withdrawing Dave Smith from midfield to the sweeper role which ultimately earned him Scotland's Player of the Year award that season.

Against Torino, Smith was sweeping behind Colin Jackson and eighteen-year-old Derek Johnstone as Rangers played the Italians at their own game. With Johnstone making a comfortable switch to central defence, it allowed Waddell to deploy Greig in a man-marking role on Torino's star man Claudio Sala. It was a job Greig was ideally suited to and he carried it out to perfection. As Greig recalls, Sala was marked out of the match. 'Willie used to always have pictures of the opposing team's players to show us before the game,' he says. 'He showed me a photo of Sala, said he was the danger man and told me to put him out of the game. He could see the way I was staring at the photo and he quickly added "Just for tonight Greigy, not for good".

'Well, I won the toss-up and decided to kick off. I got Alex MacDonald to play a pass to me just a little short. It gave Sala the chance to win the ball and within the first few seconds I'd gone in hard on him. I looked over at our bench and the first thing I saw was Willie Waddell sitting there shaking his head.'

Greig's uncompromising style of carrying out orders was certainly effective and Sala simply didn't want to know after that bone-jarring start. As Torino tried to get to grips with Rangers defensive set-up, the Scots gave themselves a huge boost by scoring the opening goal in the twelfth minute. Mathieson surged down the left on the counter-attack and whipped over a cross which Castellini in the Torino goal failed to hold. The ball fell into the path of Willie Johnston who despatched it first time past the helpless keeper. Half-time arrived with the Italians still trying to sort themselves out and Rangers looking comfortable with their narrow lead but the second half was a different story as a reshaped Torino finally got their attacking act together and put Rangers under all sorts of pressure. A defender was sacrificed as the home team sent on international winger Giovanni Toschi and began to stretch the Rangers defence.

But McCloy was outstanding in the visitors' goal and the immaculate Smith mopped up wave after wave of Torino attacks. However, in the sixty-fourth minute the inevitable happened and Torino equalized. Toschi fired in a shot which McCloy appeared to have covered until Pulici stuck out a boot to deflect the ball into the net, despite Jackson's efforts to clear it off the line.

Desperate defending by Torino as Rangers pile on the pressure at Ibrox in the quarter-final, second leg.

The Italians frantically pushed forward for a winner but the closest they came was when another Pulici effort was disallowed for offside. Rangers had pulled off a terrific result and were on the threshold of the semi-finals. A proud Waddell singled out teenager Johnstone for special praise and said, 'The Italian fans must have been amazed at him, a player who can be the new John Charles.'

Deflated Torino coach Gustavo Giagnoni wasn't about to disagree with Waddell's verdict on the quality of his team's defensive performance. Giagnoni said, 'Rangers came here and played the Italian game. It was too defensive but it is the kind of game that Italian teams have used often when they are away from home in a European tie and we can have no complaints.'

Waddell was looking to add to his squad before the end of the season but he failed in a bid for St Johnstone's highly rated midfielder John Connolly when the Perth club turned down his £45,000 bid. The Rangers manager did, however, have the errant Willie Henderson back in his plans when the winger returned to the Ibrox fold, two months after walking out over a contract dispute and vowing he would not be back. It was further proof, if it was needed, that when Waddell had an argument with anyone on Rangers business, there was only one winner.

On Wednesday 22 March at Ibrox, an ever more confident and expectant crowd of 75,000 turned up to see Rangers clinch their place in the last four of the Cup-Winners' Cup. Waddell, though, knew the job was only half done even though Johnston's goal in Turin had given his side the initiative. He stuck with the same team and the same formation which had frustrated the Italians a fortnight before. It was a phoney war for much of the first half until Rangers received a wake-up call when Toschi hit the post four minutes from the interval. The warning was heeded and just a minute into the second half, Rangers broke the deadlock on the night to go 2–1 ahead on aggregate. Tommy McLean skipped past full back Fosati down the right and delivered a cross which caused panic in the Torino defence. Johnston went up with Castellini to challenge for the ball and managed to flick it on. Alex MacDonald, running in unmarked at the back post, knocked the ball into the empty net with his knee. It was hardly a classic strike but that was of no consequence to Rangers or their supporters. Torino's spirit was broken and they were fortunate not to concede more goals in a second half controlled by the Ibrox men. Greig and Johnston both hit the woodwork while a Johnstone header was cleared off the line.

Rangers went into the semi-final draw along with Bayern Munich, Dinamo Berlin and Moscow Dynamo. Almost inevitably, they were paired with their old foes from Germany. After defeat in both the 1967 Cup-Winners' Cup Final and the first round of the Fairs Cup in 1970, Rangers were looking to make it third time lucky against the brilliant Bavarians.

The first leg was just a fortnight after the Torino tie and before they headed for Germany, Rangers had mixed fortunes on domestic business. An embarrassing home defeat by Morton finally suffocated any hopes of a late revival in the championship. 'I always felt if we could have played in the domestic games with the same tactics we employed in Europe, then we would have won the league,' claims McCloy. 'But the emphasis on Rangers at home is always to attack and, understandably I suppose, he wasn't prepared to change that.' Waddell's men nonetheless ensured they travelled to Munich in good spirits by beating Motherwell 4–2 at Ibrox in their Scottish Cup replay to book a place in the semi-finals.

To say Bayern had a star-studded line-up at the time is a bit like saying Robert De Niro is a decent actor. Sepp Maier, Franz Beckenbauer, Paul Breitner, Gerd Muller and Uli Hoeness were all coming to the peak of their powers and would form the spine of the West German side which lifted the European Championship later that season and the World Cup two years later. Waddell knew it would require another supremely disciplined performance from his team and the same men who eclipsed Torino were sent out and asked for a repeat performance. Greig had suffered a painful injury in the Cup tie against Motherwell on the Saturday but Waddell used that to his advantage with an extraordinary piece of psychological warfare on the eve of the Bayern clash. 'I had been caught by a two-footed tackle right down my shins in the Motherwell game,' Greig recalls, 'and it was a case of live by the sword, die by the sword for me. I wasn't bleating about it. We had been training in Munich the day before the game and I was in the treatment room trying to get myself fit. My legs were a real mess, all cuts and bruises. Suddenly, the door burst open and in came Willie Waddell followed by a crowd of German journalists and photographers. I hadn't a clue what was going on. He pointed at me, turned to them and said, "That's Greig, the captain of Rangers, and he'll be playing against Bayern tomorrow night despite those injuries." I'm not sure what he was trying to prove, maybe he was trying to put the wind up the Germans in some way, but needless to say I had no choice but to play the following night!'

In front of 44,000 fans in the Grunwald Stadium on Wednesday 5 April, the Germans put Rangers under intense pressure right from the start. Muller, one of the finest penalty box strikers European football has ever seen, was being marked by Jackson while Johnstone was detailed to look after Hoeness. The Rangers defenders did their jobs well, with Smith again a revelation at sweeper, but it was remarkable that Bayern were only 1–0 in front at the break.

Muller had hit the post with a header in the eighth minute and he played a part in the breakthrough goal for the home team fifteen minutes later. Breitner played a neat one-two with 'Der Bomber' and gave McCloy, who had another outstanding match, no chance from around eight yards. 'In the first half hour over there, they just came at us in waves and waves,' says McCloy, 'and it was amazing we only lost one goal.'

Many teams would have folded under such a fierce bombardment but not Waddell's Rangers. Of all the qualities he had instilled in his team, resilience was at the top of the list. Having weathered the storm, Rangers grew in confidence and began to take the game to Bayern. Three minutes into the second half, the Scots once again utilized that precious knack they had acquired of grabbing an away goal. Stein worked his way into a good position and drove in a cross which eluded Maier and was met by the unfortunate Zobel who, in an attempt to clear, merely succeeded in heading the ball into his own net. Rangers then seized the initiative from the shell-shocked Germans and might even have won the match as Willie Mathieson twice joined the attack to force Maier into excellent saves. It was another stunning and exemplary display away from home and put Rangers within touching distance of the third European final of their history.

As they became more consumed by their hunger for success in the Cup-Winners' Cup, their domestic form suffered. On their return from Munich, Rangers could only draw 1–1 with Clyde at Shawfield and they then slipped to a 2–0 defeat at Dundee.

Four days before the second leg against Bayern, Waddell had to lift his men for the Scottish Cup semi-final against Hibs at Hampden but it proved to be a disappointing and costly encounter for Rangers, with influential captain Greig limping off injured after half an hour. He was replaced by Jim Denny and four minutes from half-time MacDonald put the Ibrox men in front. But in a tie which was an anti-climax for the 75,884 fans present, Jimmy O'Rourke grabbed a deserved equalizer for Hibs three minutes into the second half to force a replay.

Greig's injury was Waddell's biggest worry going into the second leg of the Cup-Winners' Cup semi-final against Bayern at Ibrox the following Wednesday night. Despite intensive treatment, his on-field lieutentant was unable to play this time. Waddell then sprang a major selection surprise when he named eighteen-year-old Derek Parlane as Greig's replacement for the night. Signed two years earlier from Queen's Park, Parlane had previously started just four first-team matches for Rangers. In what was one of the club's biggest games in living memory, it appeared a major gamble. But just as the inclusion of Derek Johnstone had paid dividends in the League Cup Final the previous season, so Parlane justified Waddell's faith in him. Handed the task of marking Bayern's midfield playmaker Franz Roth, Parlane thrived on the challenge.

It was a night of undiluted joy for Rangers and their fans in the 80,000 crowd as they outplayed and overpowered Bayern right from the start. Just forty-five seconds were on the clock when Rangers took the lead. Willie Johnston's cross seemed to catch Beckenbauer napping and the great man could only clear the ball as far as Derek Johnstone on the edge of the box. He knocked it into the path of Jardine and his left-foot cross-cum-shot totally deceived the static Maier as it looped lazily into the net.

The Germans never recovered as Jackson's marking job on Muller forced the striker to drop deeper and deeper in search of the ball.

With the remarkably assured Johnstone also keeping Hoeness quiet, Rangers were free of worry at the back and proceeded to play some free-flowing attacking football. In the twenty-third minute, the tie was effectively over and

Franz Beckenbauer cannot hide his dismay as Rangers dismantle Bayern Munich in the semi-final, second leg at Ibrox.

what a moment it was for European competition debutant Parlane. Johnston's corner was flicked on by Stein who outjumped Maier with a prodigous leap. The ball dropped to Parlane and the teenager reacted swiftly to crash home a shot off the underside of the crossbar. Rangers were now 3–1 ahead on aggregate and the European Cup-Winners' Cup Final beckoned.

Alex MacDonald fires in a shot as Rangers dominate against Bayern.

A minute into the second half, McCloy brilliantly touched a Hoeness shot onto a post and denied Bayern a way back into the contest. Rangers then hit cruise control as it all disintegrated for the Germans who started bickering among themselves. 'We really won that second leg easily,' says McCloy, 'and for one reason or another there was a lot of friction between their players as it went on.'

The final whistle sparked memorable scenes around the ground as Waddell and Greig leapt from the dug-out to join the celebrations. The following day, news came through from behind the Iron Curtain that Moscow Dynamo had beaten Dinamo Berlin on penalties, after the sides had finished level at 2–2 on aggregate in the other semi-final.

Moscow Dynamo had played at Ibrox the previous season in a friendly match, so they were not a completely unknown quantity to the Rangers manager. But Waddell wanted to see them in action before the 24 May final and set about the difficult task of arranging a spy trip to Moscow.

Derek Parlane celebrates his goal against the Germans with Tommy McLean.

In the meantime, Rangers had a domestic campaign to complete and on the Saturday after the Bayern triumph, a side showing five changes beat Airdrie 3–0 at Broomfield. Waddell then brought his big names back for the Scottish Cup semi-final replay with Hibs at Hampden on Monday 24 April. With Celtic waiting for the winners in the final, it was an opportunity for Rangers to set themselves up for a Cup double. But Hibs had other ideas and totally outplayed the Ibrox men who badly missed the still injured Greig. Goals from Pat Stanton and Alex Edwards earned the Easter Road men a convincing 2–0 win. Everything now rested on Europe if Rangers were not to finish a season which promised so much empty handed.

The league campaign fizzled to a finish with home defeats by 4–3 to Dunfermline and 2–1 to Hibs, before a 4–2 win, again at home, over Ayr United. 'We had a while to wait for the Cup-Winners' Cup Final and to be honest we were awful at the end of the league season,' admits McCloy. Rangers finished third in the championship table, sixteen points behind seven-in-a-row winners Celtic and six points adrift of second-placed Aberdeen.

Waddell had many concerns ahead of the biggest match of his career. First and foremost was the fitness, or lack of it, of Greig, the player he valued most of all. The captain had missed the last five games of the season with a badly damaged foot and Waddell was desperate for him to lead the team out in the Nou Camp Stadium. Colin Jackson was also causing concern, having limped out of the penultimate league match against Hibs with an ankle injury. In addition, the match fitness of his players had to be sustained during the three-week period between the end of the league season and the Cup Final so friendly matches against an Inverness Select and St Mirren were arranged.

Waddell also flew out to Spain to find a base for the team to use for the final. He chose the secluded Gran Hotel Rey Don Jaime in Casteldefells, some fifteen miles outside Barcelona.

Back in Inverness, there was cheering news for Waddell when Greig managed to play the final fifteen minutes of a testimonial match for Ally Chisholm, Ernie Latham and Chic Allan of Inverness, at Grant Street Park which Rangers won 5–2 after trailing 2–1 to their enthusiastic part-time opponents.

Waddell's next task was to update his dossier on Moscow Dynamo, who had only just started their league season, but who were playing hard to get. Communication with the Soviet Union was difficult enough at the best of times but Waddell was nothing if not persistent. After weeks of sending messages to Moscow, he finally received word that he would be able to watch Dynamo face Kairat Alma Ata in a Soviet Supreme League match in the Russian capital eight days before the Cup-Winners' Cup Final. A visa was obtained from the Soviet Embassy in London and Waddell headed behind the Iron Curtain.

After initially being told he would have to buy a ticket for the match, the Ibrox boss won the suspicious local officials round and the customary complimentary seat was provided. What Waddell saw, as Dynamo came from behind to draw 1–1, would prove invaluable. It wasn't a dazzling display by the Muscovites by any stretch of the imagination. Indeed, they were booed off the pitch by their fans at the end of the game. But Waddell now knew just how tough it was going to be for his team to lift the Cup-Winners' Cup and he had pinpointed the Dynamo danger man. Josef Sabo was a newcomer to the Dynamo ranks since Rangers had beaten them 1–0 in that Ibrox friendly eighteen months previously but Waddell now knew all about the man who had been signed from Dynamo Kiev some six months before.

Sabo had World Cup Finals experience for his country and was in the Kiev side who knocked Celtic out of the European Cup in the first round as the Parkhead men defended the trophy in the 1967–8 season. Against Kairat that night, Sabo stuck out like a sore thumb and it was no surprise when he moved into midfield from his normal sweeper role and scored Dynamo's only goal. Waddell said afterwards, 'I had seen quite a few of their players before but I had not seen the team with Sabo playing. He makes so much difference and just through his play we will have to revise some of our thoughts about the game in Barcelona. Sabo is the thermometer of the team. It is through Sabo that you can judge how things are going. He guides the way the team plays and coaxes some of the less experienced men through a game. Whether it is in defence or in attack everything seems to be controlled by that one man. It was an astonishing performance and it convinced me that he will have to be kept occupied as much as possible in Spain.

'The opposition is as difficult as I imagined it would be. No team can ever reach a European final without being a good team, without being a team that you must respect. If Moscow Dynamo were not that kind of team then they would never get close to a final in a European tournament such as this one. They looked solid in defence and their wingers, though they did not do so much in this game, proved to me that on their day they could be the types to win games almost on their own. I wanted to take a look at the wingers because I had heard about them and I am very glad that I was able to see them in this game. Both of them, the outside-right Estrekov and the outside-left Evryuzhikbin have been in the Russian national team and have been successful at that level. Another aspect of their play which I noted was that their full-backs Basalev and Dolmatov were always ready to come forward into attack. This will be as difficult a task for us as the semi-final games against Bayern Munich were.'

Running Moscow Dynamo were two vastly experienced Russian football figures – coach Konstantin Beskov and technical director Lev Yashin. Yashin, arguably the finest goalkeeper of all time, was not slow to indulge in some mind games when he met Waddell in Moscow. He was keen to point out that Rangers were hot favourites as they had eliminated a far higher pedigree of sides on their way to the final. Dynamo had been fortunate, according to Yashin, to draw teams from Greece, Turkey and East Germany. He claimed their only real test had come against Yugoslavian giants Red Star Belgrade in the quarter-finals. Waddell accepted the praise politely but wasn't taken in by Yashin's comments. He knew Rangers would be facing a team hell bent on making history as the first from the Soviet Union to lift a European trophy and all the honour and privileges that would bring them in their homeland.

While Waddell was in Moscow, his assistant Willie Thornton and coach Jock Wallace took charge of Rangers in their final warm-up game against St Mirren at Love Street. An Alfie Conn hat-trick contributed to a 5–2 win over their Second Division opponents but again the most significant factor was another fifteen-minute substitute appearance from John Greig. Jackson, though, had been unable to play and it would be a last-minute decision on the reliable stopper's fitness.

On Sunday 21 May Rangers flew out to Spain to set up camp. Following behind them were sixty chartered plane loads of supporters and thousands more making their way by car, bus, train and boat. The magnitude of the occasion for everyone connected with the club was obvious and Waddell's choice of a hotel well away from the hustle and bustle of Barcelona was a wise one. His players were isolated from the frenzied build-up to the match and were able to relax as they prepared themselves physically and mentally for their date with destiny.

'Only Waddell could have found that hotel,' smiles McCloy. 'It was a real retreat, a fortress and we were away from everything.'

The players got their first sight of the Nou Camp Stadium when they trained there on the Tuesday, just twenty-four hours before kick-off. The session was going well until a sour note was struck when Jackson, training full out to give his injured ankle a final test, pulled up in agony. He was out of the Cup-Winners' Cup Final. It was heartache for the player who had so brilliantly marked Gerd Muller out of the semi-final against Bayern Munich. It was unquestionably a blow for Waddell but he was also considerably boosted by John Greig emerging from the session fit enough to lead out the team.

The Rangers manager now had just one decision to make. Who would fill the one remaining place in his side – Andy Penman, Alfie Conn or Derek Parlane? The smart money favoured the experienced Penman, while teenager Parlane's incredible display against Bayern in the semi-final had put him in with a shout. But Waddell surprised everyone by picking neither – Conn would line up in midfield.

Moscow Dynamo also had injury problems when their main striker Vladimir Koslov ruled out with a thigh strain. This did little for the health and temper of coach Beskov who refused to speak to the Scottish media in Barcelona. Just 35,000 were inside the then 100,000 capacity Nou Camp for the match and around 30,000 of them had travelled from Scotland. Nonetheless, there was a carnival atmosphere before the kick-off as Rangers fans meandered across the playing surface and happily posed for photographs with the Spanish police. Sadly, that provided a total contrast for the mayhem which would greet the final whistle and sour Rangers' crowning glory.

Waddell's concerns over Sabo's influence were obvious and it was no surprise when Greig conceded the first free-kick of the final after just a few seconds with an uncompromising challenge on the Dynamo playmaker.

Waddell, next to Jock Wallace on the extreme right, looks on thoughtfully from the Nou Camp dug-out as club history is made by his players.

It was a nervy start from both sides and McCloy had to make the first save, comfortably holding a shot from Baidatchini. As Rangers took time to settle into their familiar pattern of play, they then received a real let-off when Baidatchini fired the ball across the face of McCloy's goal but the unmarked Jakubik failed to connect from just six yards out.

The Rangers keeper then dived to his right to gather a well-struck long-range effort from Makovikov and it was clear the Scots needed a spark to get into the game. This was provided by McLean who gave Pilgui in the Moscow goal his first test of the night with a shot which the Russian keeper dived to his left to collect. Rangers gradually assumed control after that as Smith dictated play from the back while MacDonald was the gaffer in the middle of the park.

The opening goal arrived in the twenty-fourth minute and brought with it an eruption of noise from the Rangers fans which could not have been louder had the stadium been full. McLean's free-kick into the Dynamo box was cleared just

Colin Stein holds off a Dynamo defender (above) while Dave Smith and Derek Johnstone are in the thick of aerial battle (right).

over the halfway line. Smith strode onto the ball and knocked a stunning fifty-yard pass over the advancing Moscow defence and into the path of Stein. The Rangers striker had got a vital stride ahead of his marker Zykov and lashed an unstoppable right-foot shot high past Pilgui from the six-yard line. The Russians were stunned and Rangers had the first goal which Waddell had predicted beforehand would be so crucial.

McCloy was a hero again with a brilliant save to deny Makovikov from

point-blank range as Moscow Dynamo tried to hit back quickly but Rangers were now in command and it was little more than they deserved when they made it 2–0 five minutes before half-time. Smith was the architect once again, this time surging forward deep into the Dynamo half. The Russian defenders backed off, allowing Smith to check the ball onto his left foot and deliver a gorgeous angled cross into the heart of the penalty area. This time, he picked out Johnston whose cute header from six yards totally wrong-footed Pilgui and nestled in the corner of the net.

Willie Johnston jumps between Zhukov and Basalev to head Rangers 2 – 0 in front in the Final.

Four minutes into the second half, it appeared as if the 1972 Cup-Winners' Cup Final was over as a contest when Rangers made it 3–0. McCloy, whose contributions in keeping out the opposition had been of inestimable value on the road to Barcelona, now turned into a goal provider at the other end. The Girvan giant's prodigious clearances became a trademark of his career and this one was surely the most spectacular and memorable of them all. His booming kick soared almost the length of the massive Nou Camp pitch and the ball dropped over defenders Dolmatov and Dobbonosov as they challenged with Stein on the edge of the Dynamo penalty area. It seemed as if the ball would go harmlessly through to McCloy's opposite number Pilgui but Johnston had anticipated the situation perfectly. Beating the offside trap, he strode unchallenged onto McCloy's clearance and from a position level with the penalty spot slid a low left-foot shot beyond the stunned Russian keeper. The only danger to Rangers now could be the overconfidence a three-goal lead can induce. As Greig recalls, 'I remember running over to Willie Johnston when he scored the third. He had been in the 1967 team with me and I said to him "That's it wee man, we can't lose it this time." I nearly had cause to wish I never said it.'

While Johnston and his team-mates celebrated his second goal of the match, Moscow Dynamo coach Beskov sent on Estrekov for the ineffective Jakubik. Ten minutes later, the substitute shook Rangers out of any possible complacency when he pulled a goal back. Mathieson conceded possession cheaply to Evryuzhikbin and he crossed from the right for Estrekov to give McCloy no chance from close range.

Rangers were now being forced into more defending than they would have liked but Waddell's men appeared secure enough as the clock counted down. McLean came close to easing all the worries when he fired a twenty-yard shot just over the top after good work from the industrious Stein on the counter-attack. But three minutes from time, Dynamo set up a nail-biting finale to the match when they scored again to make it 3–2.

Makovikov, the Russians' best player on the night, surged forward with the kind of energy which belied the exertions of the previous eighty-six minutes. With the Rangers defence backing off, he played a one-two with Dynamo's second substitute Gerschkovitch and slammed a high shot over McCloy and into the roof of the net. 'Even when we let it slip to 3–2,' recalls Jardine, 'I never felt we were going to lose.'

Whether the rest of the players shared Jardine's total confidence is open to debate and when the final whistle sounded, it was greeted with as much relief as joy. The Rangers fans, many of whom had experienced the disappointment of the Cup-Winners' Cup Final defeats of 1961 and 1967, poured onto the pitch to celebrate. Waddell's players were quickly engulfed by the jubilant throng and had to battle their way into the dressing room where they waited for the moment when they would be recalled onto the pitch to receive the trophy. Sadly, the call never came.

Goal heroes Stein and Johnston celebrate with Alex MacDonald.

Back on the pitch, the Spanish police were in no mood for the impromptu celebrations which were taking place. There's no doubt many of the Rangers fans were fired up by a combination of the heady triumph achieved by their team, the balmy Catalan weather and a considerable intake of San Miguel during the day but there was no warning when the Barcelona constabulary drew their batons and suddenly began wading into the light blue legions. It quickly turned ugly as many irate Rangers fans responded by removing seats from the stands and used them in retaliation to the baton attacks. As the riot continued, it quickly became evident the presentation of the trophy and medals would have to be cancelled.

'The pitch invasion and the bother between our fans and the police took the shine off it,' admits McCloy. 'The fans were only doing what they had seen other fans doing in previous European finals but the Spanish police took a different view. It was a riot that should never have started.'

Waddell was incensed that the moment he had worked so hard to achieve had been sullied by the disturbance. Skipper Greig recalls, 'He and I were taken along a corridor deep inside the stadium to a tiny room where some UEFA officials were waiting with the Cup-Winners' Cup. One of them handed the trophy to me with hardly a word and then we were on our way back to the dressing room. Willie was absolutely raging, he was totally disgusted at the manner in which the trophy was presented. It was one of the greatest nights of my career but in the end that was a real slap in the face for Rangers.'

Moscow Dynamo coach Beskov was quick to seize upon the situation, claiming afterwards his players had been intimidated by the large Rangers support and that the referee had blown the final whistle too early. He added that the Russians would be launching an appeal in the hope of either having the result overturned or the final replayed.

Rangers, though, were determined the trouble would not totally spoil their moment of glory. When Greig returned to the dressing room and held the trophy aloft for his team-mates to see, the party began. The champagne corks popped and the smile returned to Waddell's face as he joined in, taking a drink from the famous trophy. McCloy recalls how Waddell ensured the players then had a night to savour when they got back to their Castledefells base. 'Our wives and the travelling press, who had been staying elsewhere, were invited back to the hotel and Waddell gathered everyone together. He made a terrific speech, telling us it was the greatest night in the club's history and that we should be proud. He said it was a time to party and that's exactly what we did. The champagne was flowing all right. Then on the stroke of midnight, he suddenly instructed that all the women were to leave and go back to their own hotel. It was to be a private celebration after that and it went on until the next morning.

The sweet taste of European glory for MacDonald while his team-mates wait their turn.

'At the time, I think we all felt we could do it again but now all these years later, Rangers are still waiting to win a European trophy again. It really was a fair achievement, especially with a team of eleven Scots and that will never be repeated.'

Jardine agrees, saying, 'I don't think the scale of what we did has ever been fully appreciated and that takes a bit of the shine off it. We played top-quality sides from leading European countries in every round and never lost a single leg by more than one goal. When we started the campaign, all we were thinking about was qualifying for the next round. No-one really talked about winning it but we kept drawing great teams and beating them.

'We played one of the first sweeper systems used by a British club with Dave Smith doing the job. In some games we went man for man at the back, in others it was zonal marking. But it was never too tactical or complicated under Waddell. He had just done his homework well and we all knew what we had to do. The secret of our team was that he believed in the team, not individuals. The heritage of the club was everything to him, no one was allowed to think they were bigger than Rangers.'

Waddell takes a well-earned dip and soaks up the Catalan sunshine with his backroom staff.

The trophy takes pride of place as the Rangers players come to terms with the morning after the night before.

If anyone was entitled to bask in individual glory, it would have been Johnston whose two goals in the final took his tally for the tournament to four. But he says, 'While it was great for me to score two goals in a European final, we had a great team with a great spirit. Colin Stein was our top scorer in Europe with five goals but you couldn't pick one star out of the campaign. I was in the side which lost the 1967 Final and that was made all the worse for us by Celtic winning the European Cup that year. It put a lot of pressure on us in 1972 but once we had got through the second round against Sporting, when we all thought we were out, I always felt our name was maybe on the trophy.'

For the bearded Greig – he had grown it after cutting his face shaving on the morning of the Sporting Lisbon game in Glasgow and vowed not to remove it until Rangers were knocked out – it was a poignant celebration. In truth, as he freely admits, his foot injury should have ruled him out of the final but such was the bond between Waddell and himself, the manager simply had to have him out on the pitch. 'I sat in a quiet corner of the hotel that night, sipping a glass of champagne, and Willie came over to me,' Greig recalls. 'He put his arm around me and just said "We did it." I looked at him and said, "Aye, but I shouldn't have been playing gaffer." He smiled and replied, "You were playing in any

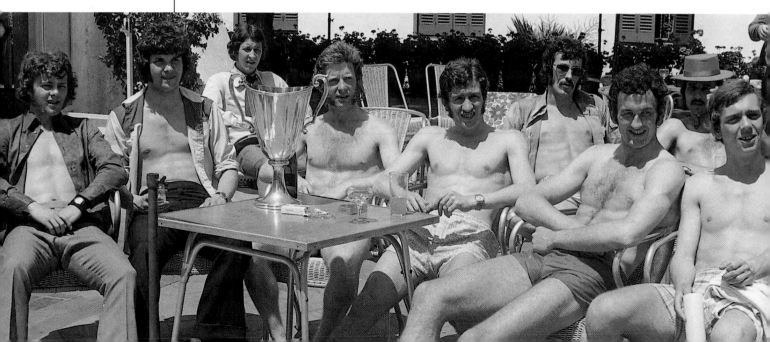

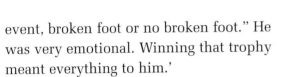

event, broken foot or no broken foot." He was very emotional. Winning that trophy meant everything to him.'

Some six cases of champagne were seen off as the Rangers management and players partied until around 5 am on the Thursday morning. After a couple of hours' sleep, they emerged tired but happy and continued the celebration with an impromptu dip in the hotel swimming pool. Even Greig jumped in which said much for how much he had enjoyed himself – he can't swim!

Torino coach Gustavo Giagnoni was a surprise visitor as he offered his congratulations to his quarter-final conquerors, a nice touch which was greatly appreciated by Waddell.

The Rangers fans, meanwhile, had been having their own all night party in downtown Barcelona but were still waiting for their first glimpse of the Cup-Winners' Cup. They got it early on Thursday afternoon at Barcelona Airport as Greig recalls. 'A lot of the supporters' planes were leaving at around the same time as our flight and I walked across the tarmac with the trophy in my hands. Suddenly, loads of our punters began to pour off their planes to try and get a glimpse of the Cup and before I knew it I was surrounded. I don't think the airport security people were too chuffed and I was hustled up the steps into our plane as quickly as they could.'

The Cup-Winners' Cup certainly had one of its most eventful journeys in Greig's hands. When the Rangers flight got back to Prestwick Airport, the Ibrox captain found himself facing one of his most difficult opponents of the whole campaign. 'It was bizarre,' he recalls, 'but I was stopped when I walked through the Nothing to Declare channel at the airport. A customs officer pointed to the trophy I was still carrying and asked me what it was. I thought he was winding

Everyone wants a taste of Waddell's success while proud chairman John Lawrence shows off the trophy.

John Greig holds the trophy aloft at a rain-soaked Ibrox on the team's triumphant return.

Greig shows the spoils of victory to the fans at Barcelona Airport as he boards the flight home.

me up at first and I just replied "It's a cup." He then asked me if I was going to declare it. When I said no, he asked me why! I said it was because I hadn't bought it and when I explained to him how I had got it, he finally let me through.'

Back in Glasgow, a crowd of 30,000 had gather at rain-lashed Ibrox to give Waddell and his players a welcome home. The squad were taken around the stadium on the back of a lorry and Greig was finally able to hoist the Cup-Winners' Cup aloft in the manner he had been deprived of in the Nou Camp.

Rangers had fulfilled the ambition they cherished above all others and less than three years after taking over as manager, Willie Waddell had restored the club's pride and credibility. It looked set to be just the start of a memorable managerial reign at Ibrox but Waddell had other ideas. Not for the first time in his career, he was about to surprise everyone with the next chapter of the Waddell years.

Waddell is given centre stage by his players, (above), while Greig crowns two-goal hero Willie Johnston, (below).

CHAPTER SEVEN
WADDELL – THE ADMINISTRATOR

WHEN RANGERS CALLED A PRESS CONFERENCE IN THE BLUE ROOM AT IBROX ON 7 JUNE 1972, two weeks after their Cup-Winners' Cup win, no one present had anticipated the dramatic announcement made by Willie Waddell. The waiting press men speculated that they would be given an update on Moscow Dynamo's appeal to UEFA that the final should be replayed because of the crowd trouble at the end of the match. Instead, Waddell walked in with Jock Wallace to drop the bombshell that he was stepping down as manager of Rangers. He was to become general manager of the club and Wallace would succeed him as team boss.

Waddell told the stunned press corps, 'We have now won the Cup-Winners' Cup but it is the future we must attend to. It is too much for one man to handle all the details involved in league and European football. That is the reason behind the change. Jock will have complete responsibility in picking the team with effect from 10 July when the players report back for pre-season training.

'The partnership between myself and Jock is terrific and I am sure he will do a good job. However, I will now have much more to do with the legislative side. I become general manager and more or less still in the number one position. There is no significance in this move beyond the need to streamline our set-up.

'I have always felt that the time to make changes is when you have success rather than wait until the changes are forced upon you. I have no fears for the team's future with Jock in charge.

'Jock is in complete charge of training, tactics and team selection and though we will be working closely I know that he will never be a puppet on a string. He is his own man and I respect him for that.'

Jock Wallace took over as team boss in the unexpected aftermath of the Barcelona triumph.

The sudden change in managerial emphasis took the Rangers players by surprise, as Barcelona hero Willie Johnston recalls. 'We were all away on holiday when he packed it in as manager,' he says, 'and I think he had had enough of the pressure of the job.'

According to Peter McCloy, no one was prepared to believe Waddell was about to take a back seat. He says, 'When he moved upstairs, it was a shock. We were pleased for Jock that he got the job but we knew that Waddell would still be a big influence as general manager. That was how it turned out. We won the Scottish Cup the following season and Waddell still played a big part. He has to take a lot of the credit for all of Rangers' success in the 1970s, including winning the league three times in four seasons in the years just after he moved upstairs.'

John Greig, who continued as an inspirational captain under Wallace, agrees. 'As general manager, he was still the boss. He didn't go to the training ground any more, he left that to Jock, but Willie Waddell signed all the players. He ran the club and had many a fall out with big Jock.'

Waddell's first task in his new role as an administrator was to handle the UEFA investigation into the Barcelona crowd trouble. He was left stunned when the governing body announced their findings and banned Rangers from European competition for two years. Moscow Dynamo had insisted the match should be replayed because of the 'crowd intimidation' of their players while Waddell replied that the trouble was a one-off incident and had no bearing on the outcome of the match. After a meeting in Brussels on 16 June, UEFA general secretary Hans Bangerter declared, 'The Control and Disciplinary Committee of UEFA, having examined the official documents and reports of Moscow Dynamo and Rangers, have decided to: (A) Reject the 'replay' appeal from Moscow Dynamo and (B) To exclude Rangers FC from participating in all UEFA club competitions for two seasons: 1972–3 and 1973–4.'

Waddell was as shattered that his team would not be able to defend their trophy as he was that they would face two years on the European sidelines. He commented, 'This is very serious for the prestige of the club and we will have an emergency board meeting.'

Few people are ever successful in appealing to UEFA. Indeed, the usual outcome is that the original fine or sanction is increased as a further slap on the wrist for impudence. But Waddell was no ordinary club administrator as he would prove time and time again. Somehow, he persuaded UEFA that their judgement had been too harsh and Rangers' ban was cut from two seasons to one.

'The aftermath to Barcelona was a bit sour, to be honest,' says Sandy Jardine, 'but Waddell handled it brilliantly. After getting the ban cut, he went out onto the pitch to speak to the fans at the start of the following season. We were all lined up behind him and he laid it on the line to the supporters that pitch invasions would not be tolerated any more.'

Waddell's success didn't stop at reducing the suspension. He had also gained further compensation for the Rangers players and supporters by being one of the innovators of the new European Super Cup. Rangers, as Cup-Winners' Cup holders, would face European Cup winners Ajax in a two-leg contest which would at least fill part of the void left by the club being denied the opportunity to defend their own trophy.

'His handling of the appeal against the European ban was superb,' says Greig, 'and no one could believe he got it reduced to a year. I know how much it hurt him that we were not allowed to defend the Cup-Winners' Cup and he put a lot of energy into trying to make up for it.'

Waddell turned the Super Cup into a gala occasion. For the first leg, at Ibrox on 16 January 1973, the flags of all the nations whose teams Rangers had played in previous European ties were paraded around the ground and a crowd of 58,000 turned up to see a brilliant Ajax side – the world club champions – led by the inimitable Johann Cruyff. Rangers played well in a fine match, Alex MacDonald cancelling out Johnny Rep's opener before the Dutch masters earned a 3–1 win with further strikes from Cruyff and Arie Haan. The following week in Amsterdam, the Scots gave another fine account of themselves in the second leg but this time were edged out 3–2 as Ajax clinched a 6–3 aggregate success.

Waddell was determined Rangers' name should remain at the forefront of European football and his next mission was to complete a task which was forced upon the club by the dreadful tragedy of 2 January 1971. At the end of a dramatic Old Firm contest at Ibrox, which saw Jimmy Johnstone head Celtic in front a minute from time only for Colin Stein to equalize for Rangers in the last few seconds, sixty-six people died and 145 were injured on Stairway Thirteen, one of the exits at the Copland Road, traditionally the 'Rangers end' of the stadium.

Although initial reports pointed to the cause of the disaster being some Rangers fans trying to make their way back up the steps when they heard the roar which greeted Stein's goal, that was later disproved. The Fatal Accident Inquiry made it clear the incident took place some five minutes after the final whistle and was caused simply by people stumbling and causing a disastrous domino effect. Fans were literally crushed to death in a tragedy which resonated all over the world.

Ibrox was one of the biggest and most famous stadiums in the world but it had

Quinton Young, yet another winger signed in the Waddell era, came to Ibrox as part of the deal which took Barcelona hero Colin Stein to Coventry City.

also become one of the least secure. The Rangers board had failed to act on previous less traumatic incidents and a terrible price was paid. As the Ibrox directors struggled to come to terms with the situation, Waddell, who was manager at the time, emerged to lead the club quite inspirationally in their darkest hour. It was the first indication that he would become a superb administrator for Rangers.

When the scale of the disaster slowly became apparent at the end of the match, Waddell and rival manager Jock Stein helped victims onto stretchers. The dressing rooms were cleared of uncomprehending players as the injured and dead were brought in. Sandy Jardine, who played in the match, recalls the way Waddell took charge of the club's response in the days that followed. 'It was dreadful, words can't describe it,' he says, 'but Waddell's strength of character throughout the whole time was incredible. I don't think anyone else could have handled that situation like Willie Waddell did. When we came into the ground on the Monday morning, he had everything organized.'

Waddell had quickly contacted the Scottish League to postpone Rangers' next fixture, a game against Cowdenbeath in Fife, as well as the reserve-team fixture scheduled for Ibrox. A midweek trip to Spain to play a friendly match against Valencia was also called off. 'It would be unfair to ask the players and public to attend any Rangers football match under these circumstances,' he told the press. 'We feel the players are under a terrific strain. They, like everyone else, have been greatly grieved and affected.

'Our next game will be on 16 January against Dundee United at Ibrox. We feel that the place to restart is Ibrox Stadium. We will be holding two minutes silence before the game. In the circumstances, we would not like to subject any other club's venue to such an ordeal.'

Waddell put the Rangers players into groups and sent them to visit all of the injured in the Victoria and Southern General Hospitals. Grim faced and wearing black ties, they spent more than an hour touring the wards. At a five-hour emergency Rangers board meeting on the Monday, Waddell took control. He emerged to announce that Rangers would be making the first donation of £50,000 to an Ibrox Disaster Fund for the victims and their families. The Rangers manager also stated the club would be represented at every one of the sixty-six funerals and set about detailing squads of players to attend. 'Rangers will do everything possible to help,' he declared and he was as good as his word. Funds were also raised by a special match at Hampden where Scotland took on an Old Firm select eleven which included guest players Peter Bonetti, Bobby Charlton and George Best.

At the subsequent inquiry into the disaster, Rangers were roundly criticized and Waddell was the only club official to emerge with any credit. He resolved there and then to turn Ibrox into one of the most modern stadia in Europe, a fitting memorial to the sixty-six lives lost. 'The stadium everyone sits in now is Waddell's biggest achievement,' says Jardine, 'and it is a fitting tribute to the man's contribution to Rangers.'

Waddell had played in the days when six-figure crowds at Scottish matches were commonplace but he knew those times had gone forever. He began to travel around Europe, examining the most up-to-date stadia in leading countries like Spain, Germany and Italy. He finally settled on the Westfalen Stadium, the home of Borussia Dortmund which was being renovated for the 1974 World Cup Finals, as the role model for his new Ibrox. The Westfalen had four covered rectangular stands which tightly surrounded the playing surface, and was widely regarded as the safest and most modern venue in Germany. It took time and money but Waddell was determined it would be done in Govan.

In 1977 Waddell announced his plan to completely transform Ibrox on three sides, leaving only the famous Archibald Leitch-designed Main Stand intact. The parabolic banks of terracing would be cleared away to be replaced by three rectangular stands. In August 1978, the removal of the east terracing – where the infamous Stairway Thirteen had been – took place and a year later, the new Copland Road Stand was completed. The west terracing was the next to go and in August 1980 the new Broomloan Road Stand was officially opened when Arsenal paid a visit. The old Centenary Stand was demolished and replaced by the third, and biggest, rectangular all-seated part of the ground, and renamed

> **'Even though Jock Wallace had become the manager, Waddell still made the big decisions as far as money was concerned.'**

the Govan Stand. Waddell's vision was completed on 22 December 1981 when Liverpool travelled north for the opening of the new 44,500 capacity Ibrox Stadium. Waddell also ensured Rangers were one of the first clubs in Britain to install undersoil heating.

In just over ten years since the Ibrox Disaster, he had transformed the ground into arguably the finest in the United Kingdom. Since then, further improvements have been made, but whatever shape or form Ibrox takes, it will always owe everything to Waddell's energy and vision.

When Waddell stepped into the general manager's role, he retained sole responsibility for negotiating wages, contracts and bonuses. The talks were often one-way, as his players recall. 'Even though Jock Wallace had become the manager, Waddell still made all the big decisions as far as money was concerned,' says Johnston. 'You didn't get a lot out of him. He would do anything to save money for Rangers. He used to cut up the carbolic soap for the bath in the dressing room and go around switching off lights after people. He was incredible that way. I was up and down the stairs to his office like a yo-yo looking for money but he always came out on top.'

Peter McCloy agrees, 'It was always difficult to get anything out of him. He called the shots. I remember before the second leg of the Cup-Winners' Cup semi-final against Bayern Munich, I was just getting ready to go out and he pulled me by the jersey. He said "If we don't lose a goal tonight, we are in the final" and went on to say that if I kept a clean sheet, I would be rewarded for it. I remembered the conversation and at the start of the next season, when he was general manager, I went to see him. I reminded him what he had said and asked him for a rise. He seemed to have lost his memory all of a sudden! Despite what he'd said to me before the game, it took me a month of haggling before I got something extra.'

Rangers players of that era were notoriously poorly paid, in relative terms, and commanded nothing like the salaries enjoyed by the stars of the current era. There's little doubt Waddell believed it was an honour simply to play for the club. 'He told you what you were getting and when you look back on it, players then were completely underpaid,' says John Greig. 'But then I don't think the players today enjoy their football as much as we did. Money wasn't the thing that drove us on, which was just as well really!'

Sandy Jardine's favourite story about Waddell's fiscal policy at the Ibrox helm came from Greig's first season as manager of the club in 1978 when Rangers made impressive progress in the European Cup. 'We played Juventus in the first round,' recalls Jardine, 'and they had nine of the Italian World Cup squad in their side. We had lost the first leg 1–0 in Turin but we beat them 2–0 at Ibrox to knock them out. It was a great performance – you can imagine how a result like that for a Scottish team would be received today. Well, we received a bonus of £150 each. The players were all up in arms about it and asked if we could see "The Deedle" in the dressing room. We were all fired up and ready to face him because we felt sure even he couldn't argue with us on this one. He came in, picked up a chair, turned it round and straddled it. On went his spectacles and slid down to the end of his nose which was always the sign he was ready for a good old row. I can still remember it now. He said, "Right lads, what are we wanting to chat about today then?" Of course, he knew exactly what it was.

'We went through it all and just about everyone in the squad had their say. Waddell was a brilliant debater but on this occasion he was finding it hard and it looked as though we had backed him into a corner. Then Alex Miller played what he thought was our trump card when he said, "And what about the crowds these European Cup ties are pulling in for the club?" Well, that was the moment "The Deedle" had been waiting for and he pounced. He went into a lecture about how much it cost to run a major football club and all the expenses involved in staging a big European game. By the time he finished, he had us feeling we should be paying him for playing in Europe. He still gave us an extra £50 each, mind you, and although it wasn't anywhere near what we were looking for I think we were all fairly pleased.'

On another occasion a group of players knocked on his door to complain about their allocation of complimentary match tickets being cut. They had barely stepped inside his office before they were sent quickly on their way by Waddell who said, 'If you want tickets, you can bloody buy them like everybody else.'

Waddell was a shrewd transfer market operator. In his first season as general manager the club sold Barcelona goal heroes Colin Stein and Willie Johnston to

Coventry City and West Bromwich Albion respectively. Rangers received £90,000 plus winger Quinton Young for Stein and the following week defender Tom Forsyth was snapped up from Motherwell for just £40,000 as Wallace was given the go-ahead to reshape the side.

Waddell, though, had initially been against the sale of Johnston, whose latest disciplinary problem, a sending off against Partick Thistle in September 1972, had seen him handed a mammoth nine-week suspension by the SFA. 'When I got the ban, I decided I had to leave Scotland,' says Johnston, 'but Waddell

didn't want me to go. He was adamant about it. He offered me a six-year contract, which was incredible for me as I was twenty-five at the time. I told him there was no way I could sign it and I turned him down. He was furious and said he would make sure I didn't get a brass farthing if I did leave. Eventually, the move to West Brom went through. He was unhappy with me but, typical of the man, he didn't hold it against me.'

Rangers continued their progress on the field and Wallace's first season as manager was marked by the capture of the Scottish Cup for the first time since 1966. The game was a classic encounter with Celtic, who had held off a creditable Rangers challenge in the league to clinch their eighth successive title by a point. In a game which ebbed and flowed from start to finish, Forsyth was the unlikely hero as his first goal for the club sealed a 3–2 win for Rangers.

During the summer of 1973, John Lawrence retired as Rangers chairman. The

Colin Stein finds the net against Celtic. Old Firm superiority held the key to Rangers regaining their status as Scotland's leading club.

Alfie Conn (No. 10), who would later become a Celtic player, turns away to aclaim an Old Firm goal.

position went to vice-chairman Matt Taylor but there was little doubt who wielded the most power and influence at Ibrox now. Waddell was the club spokesman on any issue and he relished the position. Often a confrontational figure, he liked nothing better than getting into a heated debate on any subject concerning Rangers, whether it was with his players or members of the media. On one famous occasion, he threw Martyn Lewis, now one of the BBC's leading lights, down the marble stairs at Ibrox when the unfortunate reporter tried to get into a press conference from which Waddell had banned the broadcast media.

'He was very defensive of the club's name,' says Greig, 'he would fight to the death for it. He would have it out with people, he never let a disagreement fester. In fact, he deliberately looked for arguments. If things were going along smoothly, he didn't like it and he would start a row. I saw him giving press men a real going over but the next day he would be talking to the same guy as if nothing had happened.'

The goal of Waddell and Wallace now was to end Celtic's monopoly of the league title but they would have to wait. The 1973–4 season was one of transition and ended without a trophy. Celtic made it nine in a row, winning the championship by four points from Hibs with Rangers a further point behind in third place. Rangers lost out to Celtic in the semi-final of the League Cup and made early exits in the Scottish and Cup-Winners' Cups, therefore failing to qualify for Europe.

But 1974–5, the last season of the old First Division before reconstruction and

John Greig with the Scottish Cup (above) and the League Championship trophy (right) as Wallace enjoys success as Rangers manager.

the advent of the ten-club Premier Division, finally delivered what Waddell and Wallace desired most of all. Alfie Conn was sold to Spurs for a healthy fee of £140,000 and £40,000 of that was used to sign Bobby McKean from St Mirren and goalkeeper Stewart Kennedy was snapped up from Stenhousemuir for just £10,000. Waddell scored another transfer market coup in re-signing Colin Stein from Coventry City two months from the end of the season as the Highfield Road club were unable to keep up the payments on the original deal. Rangers romped to their first championship for ten years and it was Stein who scored the goal at Easter Road on 29 March 1975 in a 1–1 draw with runners-up Hibs which won the title.

The transformation in Rangers' fortunes, started by Waddell's return to the club six years earlier, was blooming and in 1975–6 it blossomed delightfully for Jock Wallace. Rangers retained their title, becoming the first Premier Division champions, and added the League Cup and Scottish Cup to complete the third 'Treble' in Ibrox history. The season also saw Waddell become vice-chairman as well as general manager.

At the start of the 1976–7 season Waddell linked up with big-money sponsorship for the first time as Rangers successfully staged the Tennent Caledonian Cup at Ibrox. Southampton, Hearts and Partick Thistle took part with the English FA Cup holders beating Rangers in a final watched by 40,000 fans. However, the rest of the season was a major disappointment as Rangers surrendered all three trophies won in the previous campaign and went out of the European Cup in the first round.

Waddell's reaction was to spend a six-figure sum on a player who would become a true Ibrox legend. He had always loved wingers and both he and Wallace were big fans of Davie Cooper, who had starred against Rangers for Clydebank in four League Cup matches that season. Cooper had turned down numerous offers to leave Kilbowie as he was happy and content with his lifestyle at the unfashionable family-run club. But he was persuaded to join Rangers as Waddell paid the Bankies £100,000 – arguably the best £100,000 Rangers have ever spent. Along with Gordon Smith, purchased from Kilmarnock for £65,000, Cooper revitalized Rangers and in the 1977–8 season the Treble was won for the second time in three seasons.

Rangers were unquestionably Scottish football's team of the 1970s and

Waddell pulls the jersey on once more for an old-timers reunion.

John Greig seals another Scottish Cup success with a kiss.

The League Championship trophy is back in Ibrox hands, (above), and Wallace enjoys the second Treble of his managerial career, (right).

the Waddell-Wallace combination appeared unshakeable. But on 23 May 1978, just over two weeks after the Treble had been clinched with a 2–1 defeat of Aberdeen in the Scottish Cup Final, Jock Wallace sensationally resigned as manager of Rangers and moved to Leicester City, refusing to give the reason for his departure. Rumours were rife of a fall-out with Waddell and it was speculated that the general manager had blocked bids by Wallace to sign a number of players, including Alan Hansen, Andy Gray and David Narey. What was indisputable was that despite all the due and proper credit Wallace received for the trophies he delivered to Rangers,

Waddell remained firmly in overall charge.

Rangers acted quickly in appointing a successor to Wallace and it was Waddell, who now held the title of managing director, who made the choice. John Greig was named manager twenty-four hours after Wallace's departure and the captain went straight from the dressing room to the manager's room at the end of a glorious playing career.

There was clearly a deep affinity between Waddell and Greig and he desperately wanted his former captain to succeed in the new role. 'I felt from an early age he saw in me someone similar to himself,' says Greig, 'someone who could carry on the traditions of the club. There's no doubt that is why, when Jock Wallace left and it was the end of my career on the pitch, I was appointed manager.'

Sandy Jardine and John Greig milk the moment as Rangers clean up the domestic trophies in 1978.

Greig's first season was satisfying enough. The League Cup and Scottish Cup were both retained and the championship was lost to Celtic only in the last five minutes of a dramatic decider against Celtic at Parkhead. Rangers were beaten 4–2. An impressive run to the last eight of the European Cup, dismissing the cream of Italy and Holland in Juventus and PSV Eindhoven with superb tactical performances, also suggested Greig could be a major success.

But the 1979–80 season proved a disaster for Greig and Rangers, and a pivotal one in the influence Waddell held over the club. On 25 September 1979 Waddell unexpectedly announced he was stepping down as both vice-chairman and managing director of the club. Rangers made a statement which read: 'Mr Willie Waddell has requested to be relieved of his executive duties and has tendered his resignation as managing director and vice-chairman of Rangers Football Club. After more than forty years in football, both as a player and administrator, Mr Waddell wishes to be freed from the unrelenting pressures of day-to-day management. The board, in respecting his wishes, have accepted his resignation from these positions with sincere regret but are happy to say that Mr Waddell will remain as a director and as a consultant to the club.

'The chairman, Mr Rae H Simpson, and his fellow directors pay tribute to Mr Waddell's individually outstanding service and total commitment to the Rangers

Football Club and, with his help, look forward to the future with confidence.'

Waddell revealed that he had actually handed in his resignation on the eve of the Cup-Winners' Cup tie against Fortuna Dusseldorf at Ibrox the previous week. The rest of the board asked for time to consider it but it was patently obvious Waddell had made up his mind and they were forced to accept his decision. 'I have felt the strain for some time,' Waddell told the press, 'and I decided this was the time to go. There is no disharmony. I have been at it too long and I'm feeling that I'm just about burned out. I have always maintained that football is a young man's game and I feel the club is in good hands.' Waddell had been working a fourteen-hour day, seven days a week, for Rangers since his return to the club and it had taken its toll.

Asked what his greatest achievement at Rangers had been, he surprised everyone by not saying it was winning the Cup-Winners' Cup. 'I was just a part of winning that trophy in Barcelona,' he said, 'and if I have a greatest achievement, it is in bringing back the pride into the club.'

His decision greatly saddened Greig who had come to set great store by Waddell's input. 'We became very close,' says Greig, 'and it disappointed me that he decided to resign not long after giving me the job as manager. I was upset he felt he had to step back because his influence was important for me.'

Although Waddell was retained on a consultant basis, and oversaw the completion of the revamped Ibrox Stadium, he left a void Rangers found impossible to fill. On the pitch, things suffered badly. They finished fifth in the Premier Division in the 1979–80 season, their worst performance in fifteen years, crashed out of the League Cup in the third round and lost to Celtic after extra-time in a Scottish Cup Final marred by a violent pitch invasion. The following season, a superb 4–1 win over Dundee United in the replayed Scottish Cup Final gave renewed hope of a successful era under Greig but it was a false dawn.

In June 1981, Willie Waddell left his £15,000-a-year post as consultant but remained as a director. It was the end of an era. Greig delivered the League Cup the following season but a barren 1982–3 and a poor start to the subsequent campaign led to his resignation as manager in October 1983. No one was more dismayed than Waddell who, as he had done in the case of Scot Symon some sixteen years before, felt such a great servant as Greig should not have been allowed by the board to sever his ties with Ibrox completely. Waddell was therefore delighted when Greig returned to Rangers as their Public Relations Officer six years later. 'He was a big influence on my career and on the rest of my life,' says Greig. 'After I left the club, he used to phone me regularly and he would be on for an hour at a time to see how I was. He was delighted when I came back and I was glad he was alive to see that. He felt I shouldn't have been allowed to leave in the first place and he really was delighted that I was back at the club.'

On 20 December 1984 Waddell severed his last official link with Rangers when he resigned as a director. He was given the title of honorary director and was a regular visitor to Ibrox until his sudden death from a heart attack on 14 October

1992 at the age of seventy-one. Tributes poured in for the man whose impact on Scottish football in so many different ways bears few comparisons. Among them was one from then Celtic chairman Kevin Kelly who said, 'He was one of Scotland's greatest football heroes. We knew him as a player, manager and director and respected him as a hard but fair rival.'

Waddell's funeral at Linn Crematorium in Glasgow was attended by former team-mates, most of his Cup-Winners' Cup winning side and representatives from all corners of the game. Graeme Souness, who had resigned as manager of Rangers the previous year, was among the mourners and a wreath laid by the then Liverpool boss showed that even in his later years, Waddell's counsel was still being sought by the man in the Ibrox hot seat. It said simply, 'To Willie: A good friend and confidant.'

'He has to be held up in the highest regard. No one has done more for Rangers.'

No matter what Rangers achieve in the future, it is unlikely any single individual will contribute as much to the club as Willie Waddell. 'He was a one-off, I've never come across anyone like him in football. Everything was second to Rangers for "The Deedle",' says Sandy Jardine.

Peter McCloy summed up the man by saying, 'He had a vision of the game on and off the pitch. Somehow he managed to be both forward thinking and very traditional at the same time.' In John Greig's view, 'He has to be held up in the highest regard. No one has done more for Rangers.'

As a permanent reminder of the Rangers player, manager and administrator, one of the hospitality suites inside Ibrox is called The Waddell Suite. But one suspects that as long as Ibrox Stadium is standing, it will remain the perfect memorial to the one man who came closest of all to disproving Bill Struth's maxim that no individual is bigger than the club. Willie Waddell was, quite simply, Mr Rangers.

STATISTICS

Born: Forth, Lanarkshire, 7 March 1921.
Signed professional forms for Rangers in March 1938.

Rangers Playing Career

1938–9	Scottish League	27 appearances	7 goals
	Scottish Cup	2 appearances	0 goals
	Other matches	3 appearances	2 goals
1939–40	Scottish League	5 appearances	2 goals
	Wartime competitions	36 appearances	6 goals
1940–41	Wartime competitions	18 appearances	6 goals
1941–2	Wartime competitions	29 appearances	11 goals
1942–3	Wartime competitions	44 appearances	12 goals
1943–4	Wartime competitions	32 appearances	8 goals
1944–5	Wartime competitions	42 appearances	20 goals
1945–6	Wartime competitions	52 appearances	25 goals
1946–7	Scottish League	22 appearances	5 goals
	Scottish Cup	3 appearances	0 goals
	League Cup	7 appearances	2 goals
	Other matches	2 appearances	0 goals
1947–48	Scottish League	12 appearances	2 goals
	Scottish Cup	3 appearances	1 goal
	League Cup	7 appearances	0 goals
	Other matches	4 appearances	0 goals
1948–9	Scottish League	20 appearances	3 goals
	Scottish Cup	5 appearances	0 goals
	League Cup	8 appearances	4 goals
	Other matches	2 appearances	0 goals
1949–50	Scottish League	7 appearances	4 goals
	Scottish Cup	3 appearances	0 goals
	League Cup	9 appearances	4 goals
	Other matches	3 appearances	1 goal
1950–51	Scottish League	28 appearances	6 goals
	Scottish Cup	2 appearances	1 goal
	League Cup	6 appearances	0 goals
	Other matches	3 appearances	1 goal
1951–2	Scottish League	24 appearances	5 goals
	Scottish Cup	3 appearances	1 goal
	League Cup	10 appearances	2 goals
	Other matches	7 appearances	0 goals

1952–3	Scottish League	16 appearances	2 goals
	Scottish Cup	5 appearances	0 goals
	League Cup	9 appearances	1 goal
	Other matches	3 appearances	0 goals
1953–4	Scottish League	29 appearances	3 goals
	Scottish Cup	6 appearances	1 goal
	League Cup	8 appearances	2 goals
	Other matches	15 appearances	1 goal
1954–5	Scottish League	11 appearances	0 goals
	Scottish Cup	0 appearances	0 goals
	League Cup	4 appearances	0 goals
	Other matches	4 appearances	2 goals
1955–6	No League or Cup appearances		
	Other matches	1 appearance	0 goals

Career Totals

Scottish League	201 appearances	39 goals
Scottish Cup	32 appearances	4 goals
League Cup	68 appearances	15 goals
Other matches	47 appearances	7 goals
Wartime competitions	253 appearances	88 goals
Total	601 appearances	153 goals

Honours Won as a Player

League Championship	1938–9, 1946–7, 1948–9, 1952–53
Scottish Cup	1948–9, 1952–3
Scottish Regional League	1939–40
Southern League Championship	1942–3, 1943–4, 1944–5, 1945–6
Scottish Emergency War Cup	1939–40
Southern League Cup	1941–2, 1942–3, 1944–5
Summer Cup	1941–2
Victory Cup	1945–6
Glasgow Cup	1939–40, 1943–4, 1944–5, 1949–50, 1953–54
Charity Cup	1938–9, 1939–40, 1941–2, 1943–4, 1944–5, 1945–6, 1950–51

Waddell was capped seventeen times for Scotland in full official internationals, scoring six goals.

Managerial Career

KILMARNOCK FC

1957–8	Scottish League	fifth
	Scottish Cup	third round
	League Cup	quarter-finalists
1958–9	Scottish League	eighth
	Scottish Cup	quarter-finalists
	League Cup	semi-finalists

1959–60	Scottish League	runners-up
	Scottish Cup	runners-up
	League Cup	first round
1960–61	Scottish League	runners-up
	Scottish Cup	second round
	League Cup	runners-up
1961–2	Scottish League	fifth
	Scottish Cup	quarter-finalists
	League Cup	first round
1962–3	Scottish League	runners-up
	Scottish Cup	second round
	League Cup	runners-up
1963–4	Scottish League	runners-up
	Scottish Cup	semi-finalists
	League Cup	first round
1964–5	Scottish League	champions
	Scottish Cup	quarter-finalists
	League Cup	first round
	Fairs Cup	second round

RANGERS FC

1969–70	Scottish League	runners-up
	Scottish Cup	quarter-finalists
1970–71	Scottish League	fourth
	Scottish Cup	runners-up
	League Cup	winners
	Fairs Cup	first round
1971–2	Scottish League	third
	Scottish Cup	semi-finalists
	League Cup	first round
	European Cup-Winners' Cup	winners

MANAGERIAL TOTAL IN CHARGE OF RANGERS

Scottish League: played 87, won 47, drew 15, lost 25. Goals for: 165. Goals against: 95.
Scottish Cup: played 17, won 9, drew 5, lost 3. Goals for: 37. Goals against: 19.
League Cup: played 16, won 13, drew 1, lost 2. Goals for: 36. Goals against: 8.
European competition: played 11, won 5, drew 4, lost 2. Goals for: 17. Goals against: 13.
Total: played 131, won 74, drew 25, lost 32. Goals for: 255. Goals against: 135.

THE ROAD TO BARCELONA – THE EUROPEAN CUP-WINNERS' CUP, 1971–2

15 September 1971. First round, first leg.
RENNES 1 (Redon 78)   RANGERS 1 (Johnston 68)
Rennes: Auboir, Cosnard, Cedolin, Chlosta, Cardiet, Garcia (Redon), Keruzore, Terrier, Mosjov, (Periault), Betta, Lenoir.
Rangers: McCloy, Jardine, Mathieson, Greig, McKinnon, Jackson, McLean, MacDonald, Stein (Denny), Penman, Johnston.
Attendance: 20,000.

28 September 1971. First round, second leg.
RANGERS 1 (MacDonald 38)   RENNES 0
Rangers: McCloy, Jardine, Mathieson, Greig, McKinnon, Jackson, Henderson, Conn, Stein, MacDonald, Johnston.
Rennes: Auboir, Cosnard, Cardiet, Cedolin, Chlosta, Toublant, Terrier, Garcia, Keruzore (Redon), Betta, Lenoir.
Attendance: 40,000.   Rangers won 2–1 on aggregate.

20 October 1971. Second round, first leg.
RANGERS 3 (Stein 9, 19; Henderson 28)   SPORTING LISBON 2 (Chico 70, Gomes 86)
Rangers: McCloy, Greig, Mathieson, Jardine, McKinnon, Smith, Henderson, Penman (Conn), Stein, Fyfe, MacDonald.
Sporting Lisbon: Damas, Laranjiero (Lourenco), Hilario, Goncalves (Gomes), Calo, Jose Carlos, Chico, Nelson, Yazalde, Vagner, Dinis.
Attendance: 50,000.

3 November 1971. Second round, second leg.
SPORTING LISBON 4 (Yazalde 26, Tome 37, Gomes 83, Perez 114)
RANGERS 3 (Stein 27, 46; Henderson 100)
Sporting Lisbon: Damas, Gomes, Hilario, Tome, Talo, Laranjiero, Vagner, Lourenco, Yazalde, Perez, Dinis (Marinho).
Rangers: McCloy, Greig, Mathieson, Jardine, McKinnon (Smith), Jackson, Henderson, Conn, Stein, Johnston (McLean), MacDonald.
Attendance: 60,000.   Aggregate 6–6; Rangers won on away goals.

8 March 1972. Quarter-final, first leg.
TORINO 1 (Toschi 61)   RANGERS 1 (Johnston 12)
Torino: Castellini, Mozzini, Fossati (Toschi), Zecchin, Cereser, Agroppi, Rampanti, Ferrini, Pulici, Sala, Bui.
Rangers: McCloy, Jardine, Mathieson, Greig, Jackson, Smith, McLean, Johnstone, Stein, MacDonald, Johnston.
Attendance: 35,000.

22 March 1972. Quarter-final, second leg.
RANGERS 1 (MacDonald 46)   TORINO 0
Rangers: McCloy, Jardine, Mathieson, Greig, Jackson, Smith, McLean, Johnstone, Stein, MacDonald, Johnston.
Torino: Castellini, Lombardo, Fossati (Rossi), Puia, Cereser, Ferrini, Luppi, Crivelli, Bui (Barberes), Rampanti, Toschi.
Attendance: 65,000.   Rangers won 2–1 on aggregate.

---

5 April 1972. Semi-final, first leg.
BAYERN MUNICH 1 (Breitner 23)   RANGERS 1 (Zobel og 49)
Bayern Munich: Maier, Hansen, Breitner, Schwarzenbeck, Beckenbauer, Roth (Schneider), Krauthausen, Zobel, Muller, Hoeness, Suchnholz.
Rangers: McCloy, Jardine, Mathieson, Greig, Jackson, Smith, McLean, Johnstone, Stein, MacDonald, Johnston.
Attendance: 40,000.

19 April 1972. Semi-final, second leg.
RANGERS 2 (Jardine 1, Parlane 23)   BAYERN MUNICH 0
RANGERS: McCloy, Jardine, Mathieson, Parlane, Jackson, Smith, McLean, Johnstone, Stein, MacDonald, Johnston.
BAYERN MUNICH: Maier, Hansen, Breitner (Rybarczyk), Schwarzenbeck, Beckenbauer, Roth, Schneider, Zobel, Muller, Hoeness, Koppenhofer.
Attendance: 80,000.   Rangers won 3–1 on aggregate.

---

24 May 1972. Final, at Nou Camp Stadium, Barcelona.
RANGERS 3 (Stein 24, Johnston 40, 49)   MOSCOW DYNAMO 2 (Estrekov 59, Makovikov 87)
Rangers: McCloy, Jardine, Mathieson, Greig, Johnstone, Smith, McLean, Conn, Stein, MacDonald, Johnston.
MOSCOW DYNAMO: Pilgui, Basalev, Dolmatov, Zykov, Dobbonosov (Gerschkovitch), Zhukov, Baidatchini, Jakubik (Estrekov), Sabo, Makovikov, Evryuzhikbin.
Attendance: 35,000.

Appearances
9: Peter McCloy, Sandy Jardine, Willie Mathieson, Alex MacDonald, Colin Stein.
8: John Greig, Willie Johnston.   7: Colin Jackson.
6 plus 1 sub: Tommy McLean, Dave Smith.   5 : Derek Johnstone.
4: Ronnie McKinnon.   3 plus 1 sub: Alfie Conn.   3: Willie Henderson.
2 : Andy Penman.   1: Graham Fyfe, Derek Parlane.   1 sub: Jim Denny.

Goalscorers
5: Stein.   4: Johnston.   2: MacDonald, Henderson.   1: Jardine, Parlane.   1 own goal.